Spanish America

Its Romance, Reality and Future

(Volume II)

C. Reginald Enock

Alpha Editions

This edition published in 2024

ISBN : 9789361473579

Design and Setting By
Alpha Editions
www.alphaedis.com
Email - info@alphaedis.com

As per information held with us this book is in Public Domain.
This book is a reproduction of an important historical work. Alpha Editions uses the best technology to reproduce historical work in the same manner it was first published to preserve its original nature. Any marks or number seen are left intentionally to preserve its true form.

Contents

CHAPTER IX THE LANDS OF THE SPANISH MAIN COLOMBIA AND VENEZUELA .... - 1 -

CHAPTER X THE LANDS OF THE SPANISH MAIN VENEZUELA AND GUIANA .... - 14 -

CHAPTER XI THE AMAZON VALLEY IN COLOMBIA, ECUADOR, VENEZUELA, BOLIVIA, PERU, BRAZIL .... - 40 -

CHAPTER XII BRAZIL .... - 63 -

CHAPTER XIII THE RIVER PLATE AND THE PAMPAS ARGENTINA, URUGUAY AND PARAGUAY .... - 94 -

CHAPTER XIV THE RIVER PLATE AND THE PAMPAS ARGENTINA, URUGUAY AND PARAGUAY .... - 123 -

CHAPTER XV TRADE AND FINANCE .... - 146 -

CHAPTER XVI TO-DAY AND TO-MORROW .... - 156 -

FOOTNOTES: .... - 183 -

CHAPTER IX
THE LANDS OF THE SPANISH MAIN
COLOMBIA AND VENEZUELA

A sea-wall of solid masonry, a rampart upon whose flat top we may walk at will, presents itself to the winds and spray that blow in from the Gulf of Darien upon the ancient city of Cartagena, and the booming of the waves there, in times of storm, might be the echo of the guns of Drake, for this rampart was raised along the shore in those days when he and other famous sea rovers ranged the Spanish Main, over which Cartagena still looks out.

Cartagena was a rich city in those days, the outlet for the gold and silver and other seductive matters of New Granada, under the viceroys, and the buccaneers knew it well, this tempting bait of a treasure storehouse and haven of the Plate ships. This, then, was the reason for the massive sea-wall, one of the strongest and oldest of the Spanish fortifications of the New World, which Spain had monopolized and which the sea rovers disputed.

There is a certain Mediterranean aspect about Cartagena, which was named by its founder, the Spaniard, Pedro de Heredia, in 1533, after the Spanish city of Carthage, founded by the Phœnicians of the famous Carthage of Africa. The steamer on which we have journeyed has crossed the American Mediterranean, as the Caribbean has been not altogether fancifully termed, for there is a certain analogy with the original, and passing the islands and entering the broad channel brings into view the ancient and picturesque town, with the finest harbour on the northern coast of the continent, a smooth, land-locked bay, with groups of feathery palms upon its shores.

Backed by the verdure-clad hills—whereon the better-class residents have their homes, thereby escaping the malarias of the littoral—the walls and towers of the town arise, and, entering, we are impressed by a certain old-world dignity and massiveness of the place, a one-time home of the viceroy and of the Inquisition. There are many memories of the past here of interest to the English traveller. Among these stands out the attempt of Admiral Vernon, in 1741, who with a large naval force and an army—under General Wentworth—arrived expecting an outpost of the place, which Drake had so easily held to ransom, to fall readily before him. The attempt was a failure, otherwise the British Empire might have been established upon this coast.

Colombia, like Mexico, has been a land of what might be termed vanished hopes and arrested development. But the old land of New Granada, as Colombia was earlier termed, has not the weight of wasted opportunity and outraged fortune which now envelops the land of New Spain, which in our generation promised so much and fell from grace. Colombia, by a slower path, may yet reach a greater height than Mexico as an exponent of Spanish American culture.

But a century ago, at the time Colombia freed herself, in company with her neighbours, from the rule of Spain, her statesmen as well as her neighbours hailed her as a favoured land upon which fortune was to shine, which was to lead in industrial achievement, to redress the balance of the Old World, to offer liberty and opportunity to the settler, riches to the trader, to be a centre of art and thought. At that time, indeed, New Granada was the leading State in all the newly born constellation of Spanish America, and during her earlier republican period one of her orators, with that command of grandiloquent phrase with which the Spanish American statesman is endowed, spoke as follows:

> "United, neither the empire of the Assyrians, the Medes or the Persians, the Macedonian or the Roman Empire can ever be compared with this colossal Republic!"

The speaker—Zea, the vice-president—was referring to the Republic of *La Gran Colombia*, formed, under Bolivar, of Venezuela, Colombia and Ecuador—a union which was soon disrupted and which neither geography nor human politics could have done aught but tend to separate. The union, like that of Central America, fell asunder amid strife and bloodshed.

But let us take the road to Bogota, the beautiful and in many respects highly cultured capital of Colombia.

We do not, however, take the road, but the river, starting either from Cartagena by the short railway to Barranquilla, the seaport at the mouth of the Magdalena River, or direct from that port, and thence by the various interrupted stages of a journey that has become a synonym of varied travel to a South American capital.

Barranquilla is an important place—the principal commercial centre of the Republic. Here we embark upon a stern-wheel river steamer of the Mississippi type, flat-bottomed, not drawing more than three to five feet of water. The smaller boat, though less pretentious, may sometimes be the better on the long voyage upstream, and may pass the bigger and swifter craft if haply, as occurs at times, that craft be stranded on a shoal. For the river falls greatly in the dry season.

A SEAPORT ON THE AMERICAN MEDITERRANEAN, SANTA MARTA, COLOMBIA.

Vol. II. To face p. 14.

Journeying thus, we reach La Dorada, six hundred miles upstream, in about nine days, for there are many obstacles against time on the way, such as the current, the taking-in of fuel, the sand bars, which prohibit progress by night, slow discharge of merchandise and so forth. The heat may be stifling. A gauze mosquito bar or net is among the equipment of the prudent traveller, as is a cot or hammock, and rugs against the chill and damp of the nights. Also food, for the commissariat on board often leaves much to be desired. In Colombia the traveller requires clothing both light and heavy, as indeed in almost all Spanish American countries. Quinine, moreover, must always be among his equipment.

At Puerto Berrio, five hundred miles up the river, a railway runs to the interesting city of Medellin, in the mountains, the second city in importance in Colombia.

There are, from La Dorada, various changes to be made before Bogota is reached. We must change to the railway that runs to—near—Honda, circumventing the rapids, a line about twenty miles long. Here we have a choice of routes and methods. We may proceed on mule-back through magnificent scenery and the refreshing atmosphere of the Andes, with tolerable inns, or we may take the steamer again to Giradot, on the Upper Magdalena, and then a further trajectory of eighty miles by rail. Seven changes are necessary in this journey from Cartagena to the capital—ocean-steamer to train, thence to river-steamer, from that to the train again, thence to river-steamer once more, thence to the train, and again to another train—doubtless a record of varied travel.

The remote and famous city of Santa Fé de Bogota, founded by Quesada in 1538, the old viceregal capital of New Granada, the "Athens of South America" as some of its admirers have termed it, stands pleasingly upon its

Sabana, or upland plain—one of the largest cultivated mountain plateaux in the world—at an elevation of 8,600 feet above sea-level, higher than the famous city of Mexico. It is in the heart of the Tropics, but four degrees north of the Equator, and its equable climate, a result of the offsetting of latitude by altitude, is in many respects delightful.

Here the typical Spanish American character is stamped on the city and reflected in the life of its people, where Parisian dress rubs shoulders with the blanketed Indian. Here the aristocracy of Colombia, implanted by Spain, centres. One street may be lined with the handsome residences of the correct and elegant upper class, folk perhaps educated in foreign universities, men of the world, passing by in silk hat and frock-coat—attire beloved of the wealthy here—or in motor-car or carriage, which whirls past the groups of half-starved, half-clothed (and perhaps half-drunken) Indian or poor Mestizo folk, whose homes are in the hovels of a neighbouring street and whose principal source of entertainment is the *chicheria*, or drinking-den, such as exists in profusion. And without desiring to institute undue comparisons—for wealth and misery go side by side in London or New York, or any city of Christendom—it may be pointed out that despite the claim of Bogota to be a centre of literary thought and high culture, little more perhaps than a tenth of the population of Colombia can read and write.

There are handsome plazas, with gardens and statuary, but few imposing public buildings, although a certain simplicity is pleasing here. The streets generally are narrow, and the houses low, as a precaution against earthquake shocks. The *Capitiolio*, the building of the Legislature, is spacious and handsome. Upon a marble tablet, upon its façade, in letters of gold, is an inscription to the memory of the British Legion, the English and Irish who lent their aid to Colombia and Venezuela, under Bolivar, to secure independence from Spain a century or more ago.

The story of the British soldiers in this liberation is an interesting one.

> "With insubordination and murmurings among his own generals, decreased troops and depleted treasure, and without the encouragement of decisive victories to make good these deficiencies, the outlook for Bolivar and for the cause in which he was fighting might well have disheartened him at this time. In March, however, Colonel Daniel O'Leary had arrived with the troops raised by Colonel Wilson in London, consisting largely of veterans of the Napoleonic wars. These tried soldiers, afterwards known as the British Legion, were destined to play an all-important part in the liberation of Venezuela, and Bolivar

soon recognized their value, spending the time till December in distributing these new forces to the best advantage.

"Elections were arranged in the autumn, and on February 15, 1819, Congress was installed in Angostura. Bolivar took the British Constitution as his model, with the substitute of an elected president for an hereditary king, and was himself proclaimed provisional holder of the office. The hereditary form of the Senate was, however, soon given up."[1]

Before the Conquest Bogota was the home of the Chibchas people—Tunja was their northern capital—the cultured folk of Colombia, who, although inferior to the Incas of Peru, had their well-built towns and a flourishing agriculture and local trade, their temples of no mean structure, with an advanced religion which venerated and adored the powers of Providence as represented by Nature; who worked gold and silver and ornaments of jewels beautifully and skilfully, such things as Quesada's Spaniards coveted—a culture which knew how to direct the Indian population, but which, alas! fell before the invaders as all other early American cultures fell.

To-day, as then, the high mountains look down upon the Sabana, and the rills of clear water descend therefrom. Still the beautiful Mesa de Herveo, the extinct volcano, displays like a great tablecloth from a giant table its gleaming mantle of perpetual snow, over 3,000 feet of white drapery. Still the emerald mines of Muzo yield their emeralds, and still the patient Indian cultivates the many foods and fruits which Nature has so bountifully lavished upon his fatherland.

Colombia, like Peru or Mexico, or Ecuador or other of the sisterhood of nations in our survey, is a land of great contrasts, whether of Nature or man. The unhealthy lowlands of the coast give place to the delightful valleys of higher elevations, which in their turn merge into the bitter cold of the melancholy *paramos*, or upland passes, and tablelands of the Andes. Or the cultivated lands pass to savage forests, where roam tribes of natives who perhaps have never looked upon the face of the white man.

Every product of Nature in these climates is at hand or possible, and the precious minerals caused New Granada to be placed high on the roll of gold-producing colonies of the Indies. The coffee of the lowlands, the bananas, shipped so largely from the pretty port of Santa Marta, the cotton, the sugar and the cocoa, grown so far mainly for home consumption; the coconuts, the ivory-nuts—*tagua*, or *coróza*, for foreign use in button-making largely—the rice, the tobacco, the quinine, of which shipments have been considerable; the timber, such as cedar and mahogany; the cattle and hides, the gold, silver, platinum, copper, coal, emeralds, cinnabar, lead, the iron and petroleum—such are the chief products of this favoured land.

Many of the mines and railways are under British control, but in general trade German interests have been strong, and the German has identified himself, after his custom, with the domestic life of the Republic. A rich flora, including the beautiful orchids, is found here, as in the neighbouring State of Venezuela.

Two-fifths of Colombia is mountainous territory, the plateaux and spurs of the Andes, between which latter run the Magdalena and Cauca Rivers. The roads are mule-trails, such as bring again and again before us as we experience their discomforts the fact that Colombia, in common with all the Andine Republics, is still in the Middle Ages as far as means of rural transport are concerned. Yet the landscape is often of the most delightful, and the traveller, in the intervals of expending his breath in cursing the trails, will raise his eyes in admiration of the work of Nature here.

> Especially is this the case when, in the dry season, travel is less onerous and when nothing can be more pleasing than the varying scenery. Here "dipping down into a delightful little valley, formed by a sparkling rivulet whose banks are edged with cane, bamboo and tropical trees, inter-wreathed with twining vines; there, circling a mountain-side and looking across at a vast amphitheatre where the striking vegetation, in wild profusion, is the gigantic wax-palm, that towers sometimes to a height of 100 feet; then, reaching the level of the oak and other trees of the temperate zone, or still higher at an altitude of 10,000 or 11,000 feet, the *paramos*, bare of all vegetation save low shrubs, which might be desolate were it not for the magnificent mountain scenery, with the occasional view of the glorious snow-peaks of the Central Cordillera.

> "At times the road is poor: now and then, cut into the solid rock of the mountain-side, towering sheer hundreds of feet above you, while a precipice yawns threateningly on the other side, it may narrow down to a scant yard or two in width; it may, for a short distance, climb at an angle of almost forty-five degrees, with the roughest cobble paving for security against the mules slipping; or in a stretch of alluvial soil, the ruts worn by the constant tread of the

animals in the same spot have worn deep narrow trenches, characteristic of Andean roads, against the sides of which one's knees will knock roughly if constant vigilance be not exercised; worse yet, these trenches will not be continuous, but will be interrupted by mounds over which the mules have continually stepped, sinking the road-bed deeper and deeper by the iterated stamping of their hoofs in the same hollow, till deep excavations are formed, which in the rainy season are pools filled with the most appalling mud. Such is a fair picture applicable to many a stretch of so-called road in Colombia.

"The 'hotel accommodations' on the way are poor, of course; one stops at the usual shanty and takes such fare as one can get, a *sancocho* or *arepas*, eked out with the foods prudentially brought along. It is in such passes as the Quindio, too, when one reaches the *paramos*, thousands of feet in altitude, and far above the clouds, that one experiences the rigorous *cold* of the Tropics. The temperature at night is nearly always below forty degrees; occasionally it drops to freezing-point, and one feels it all the more after a sojourn in the hot lowlands. No amount of clothing then seems adequate. Travellers will remember the bitter cold nights they have passed in the *paramos*."[2]

This bitter atmosphere is experienced, let us remember, on or near the Equator. But we are led on to the beautiful Cauca Valley perhaps, whence, if we wish, we may continue on through the pretty town of Cali, and up over the tablelands of Popayan and Pasto, and, passing the frontier, so ride on to Quito, the capital of Ecuador—a journey which will leave us with sensations both painful and pleasurable.

TRANSPORTING MACHINERY IN THE COLOMBIAN ANDES.

Vol. II. To face p. 22.

"If you cannot withstand the petty discomforts of the trail for the sake of the ever-shifting panorama of snow-peaks, rugged mountains, cosy valleys, smiling woodlands, trim little valleys, then you are not worthy to be exhilarated by the sun-kissed winds of the Andes, or soothed by the languorous tropical moonlight of the lower lands, or to partake of the open-handed hospitality which will greet you.

"Such is the fame of the Cauca Valley that it was long known throughout Colombia simply as *the* valley, and that is now its legal name. It is the valley *par excellence*. The name is used to designate especially that stretch, about 15 to 25 miles wide and 150 miles long, where the Cauca River has formed a gently sloping plain, at an altitude of 3,000 to 3,500 feet above sea-level, between the Central and the Western Cordilleras. A little north of Cartago and a little south of La Bolsa, the two ranges hem it in. The Cauca is one of the real garden spots of the world. No pen can describe the beauty of the broad smiling valley, as seen from favourable points on either range, with its broad green pastures, yellow fields of sugar-cane, dark woodlands, its towns nestling at the foothills, the Cauca River in the midst, silvered by the reflected sun, and looking across the *lomas* of the rapidly ascending foothills, with cameo-cut country houses, topped by the dense forests of the upper reaches of the mountains, rising to majestic heights. From some places in the western range will be seen the snow-clad Huila in icy contrast to the blazing sun shining on the luxuriant tropic vegetation beneath.

"The best developed parts of the hot and temperate zones of Cundinamarca are along the Magdalena Valley and the routes of the Girardot Railway, the road to Cambao and the Honda trail. In the warmer zone there are good sugar plantations: in the temperate zone is grown the coffee so favourably known in the markets of the world under the name of Bogota: it attains its perfection at an altitude of about 5,000 feet, and nowhere else in Colombia has such careful attention been given to its cultivation. The Sabana itself, by which name the plateau of Bogota is known, is all taken up with farms and towns—there is scarcely a foot of undeveloped land. The climate is admirably adapted to the

European-blooded animals, and the gentleman-farmer of Bogota takes great pride in his stock. The finest cattle in Colombia, a great many of imported Durham and Hereford stock, and excellent horses of English and Norman descent are bred here. This is the only section in Colombia, too, where dairying on any extensive scale is carried on, and where the general level of agriculture has risen above the primitive. The lands not devoted to pasture are utilized chiefly for wheat, barley and potatoes.

"To offset bad water, the food supply is excellent, and of wonderful variety. That is one of the beauties of the climate of the Sabana. One gets all northern fruits and flowers, blooming the year round, and vegetables as well as quite a few of the tropical ones. It is an interesting sight to see tropical palms growing side by side with handsome northern trees, like oaks and firs. Some of the Sabana roads are lined with blackberries, and one gets delicious little wild strawberries; apples, pears and peaches are grown, though usually of a poor quality, not properly cultivated. Even oranges can grow on the Sabana, and from the nearby hot country they send up all manner of tropical fruits and vegetables. Then there is no dearth of good cooks: the epicure can enjoy private dinners and public banquets equal to any in the world. The one lady who reads this book will be interested to know that the servant problem is reduced to a minimum in Bogota; good domestics are plentiful and cheap—five to ten dollars a month is high pay. In the houses of the well-to-do the servants are well treated and lead happy lives; they have ample quarters of their own, centring around their own *patio*; and enough of the old patriarchal regime survives to make them really a part of the family."[3]

Descending from the mountainous part of the country, we reach, to the east, that portion of Colombia situated upon the affluents of the Orinoco, a region which we may more readily consider in our description of that great river, lying mainly in the adjoining Republic of Venezuela. Here stretch the *llanos*, or plains, and the forests which are the home of the wilder tribes, for Colombia has various grades of civilization among her folk, of which the last are these aboriginals, and the middle the patient Christianized Indians, who constitute the bulk of the working classes. These last have the characteristics, with small differences, of the Indian of the Cordillera in general, of whom I have elsewhere ventured upon some study.

In Colombia, although in some respects the Republic is pervaded by a truly democratic spirit as between class and class, power and privilege, land and education are in the hands of a small upper class. This condition does not make for social progress, and in the future may seriously jeopardize the position of that class. Wisdom here, as elsewhere in Spanish America, would advise a broader outlook. Political misrule in the past has been rampant, although revolutions of late years have been infrequent.

There are innumerable matters in Colombia which the observant traveller will find of the utmost interest, but upon which we cannot dwell here. Our way lies back to the Spanish Main, whence we take steamer along the coast to the seaports of Venezuela.

Colombia is in a unique geographical position upon the South American Continent, in that it is the only State with an Atlantic and Pacific coast; added to which is the hydrographic condition which gives the country an outlet also to the fluvial system of the Amazon, by means of the great affluents the Yapura and the Negro, as also the Putumayo—if that stream is to be regarded in Colombian territory, for the region is on the debatable ground claimed by three countries, Colombia, Ecuador and Peru.

Indeed, this portion of South America, one of the wildest parts of the earth's surface, is of great hydrographic interest, and looking at the map, we see how these navigable streams bend north, east and south, with the peculiar link of the Casiquiare "Canal" or river, uniting the fluvial systems of the Orinoco and the Amazon. (It is—but on a vaster scale—as if a natural waterway existed between the Thames and the Severn, or the Mississippi and the St. Lawrence.) This "Canal" lies but 150 miles from the Equator, a few miles from the border of Colombia, in Venezuela. Beyond, to the north-east, is Guiana, the land of Raleigh's El Dorado. Doubtless this region, in the future—far-off it may be—will become of much importance, and what is now savage woodland and danger-haunted waterways may some day be teeming with life and activity.

The conditions as regards navigability are, of course, relative in many instances here. Again, the region is not necessarily altogether an uninhabited one, for the rubber-stations have been increasing rapidly of late years.

A somewhat forbidding coast presents itself as our steamer, casting anchor, comes to rest in the waters of La Guayra, the principal seaport of Venezuela.

Here a bold rocky wall, apparently arising sheer from the sea, a granite escarpment more than a mile high, cuts off all view of the interior, and, reflecting the heat of the tropic sun, makes of the small and somewhat unprepossessing town at its base one of the hottest seaports on the face of the globe, as it was formerly one of the most dangerous from the exposure of its roadstead.

But, as if in some natural compensation, there lies beyond this rocky, maritime wall one of the most beautiful capital cities of South America—Caracas, reached by yonder railway, strung along the face of the precipice, and affording from the train a magnificent panorama of the seaport and the blue Caribbean.

La Guayra, ranged like an amphitheatre around the indentations in the precipice in which it lies, with its tiers of ill-paved streets, has nevertheless some good business houses, and the Republic expended a million pounds sterling upon its harbour works, executed and controlled by a British company.

Looking seaward from its quay walls, we may recall the doings of the old buccaneers of the Spanish Main, and of other filibusters, who from time to time have sacked the place since its founding in the sixteenth century. Upon these quays are filled bags of cocoa and coffee, and mountains of hides, brought down from the interior, and other products from plain and field and forest of the hinterland, for La Guayra monopolizes, for State reasons, much of the trade that might more naturally find outlet through other seaports.

The little railway which bears us up and beyond to Caracas winds, to gain elevation and passage, for twenty-four miles, in order to cover a distance in an air-line between the port and the capital of about six. We find ourselves set down in what enthusiastic descriptions of this particular zone love to term a region of perpetual spring; and indeed, at its elevation of 3,000 feet, the city is alike free from the sweltering heat of the coast and from the cold of the higher mountainous districts beyond.

A handsome plaza confronts us, with an equestrian statue of Bolivar. The plaza is mosaic-paved, electrically lighted, shaded by trees and, in the evening and on Sunday, the military bands entertain the people after the customary Spanish American method. Some showy public buildings, and a museum with some famous paintings are here; there are pleasing suburbs, luxurious gardens and well laid-out streets, and this high capital takes not unjustifiable pride to itself for its beauty and artistic environment and atmosphere—conditions which deserve a wider fame.

When we leave the Venezuelan capital and travel over the wide territory of the Republic, we find it is one of the most sparsely populated of the Spanish American nations. Conditions in internal development and social life are very much like those of Colombia, with highlands and lowlands, river and forest, cultivated plain and smiling valley, malarial districts and dreary uplands. We find the rudest Indian villages and the most pleasing towns: the most ignorant and backward Indian folk, the more docile and industrious Christianized labouring class, and the highly educated, sensitive and oligarchical upper class.

Again, we find the same variety of climate, products and the gifts of Nature in general. We see great plantations of coffee, especially in that fertile region of Maracaibo, which Colombia in part enjoys, and which gives its name to the superior berry there produced for export. We see broad estates, in their thousands, devoted to the production of the *cacao*, or chocolate, and similar areas over which waves the succulent and vivid green sugar-cane, whereon sugar is produced often by old-fashioned methods. These products yield returns so excellent that the growing of cotton, on the vast lands suitable thereto, are in large degree neglected, and must be regarded as an asset for the future, whenever local labour may become better organized or more plentiful.

Agriculture in this varied Republic, as in its neighbour, Colombia, has been kept backward by the same lack of labour, largely a punishment for the decimation of the labouring folk in the civil and other wars that have so often laid waste both man and land.

Maracaibo, lake and district, of which we have made mention, is in some respects a curious region. Let us look at the map. We remark a great indent on the coast of the Spanish Main. It is the Gulf of Venezuela, continuing far inland to what is termed Lake Maracaibo. The gulf is partly closed by the curious Goajira Peninsula.

From the appearance of the dwellings of the Indian on this lake-shore, the name of Venezuela, or "Little Venice," was given to the mainland here; the lake-dwellings are built on piles driven into the water. When the first Spaniards visited the coast, under Alonzo de Ojeada—on board with him was Amerigo Vespucci, the Florentine who gave his name to America—they were struck by the curious appearance of the Indian settlements, and from so accidental a circumstance was the region baptized. The same type of dwelling still characterizes the lake, and were it not for the busy and important town of Maracaibo, the traveller might almost fancy himself back in the sixteenth century, coasting with the early explorers.

Indeed, as far as the Indians of the peninsula are concerned, we might still be in these early times, for these sturdy descendants of the Caribs, whom the Spaniards came to dread, have maintained their independence to this day, and although they trade with the white folk, resist all attempts at governmental control. This is a curious circumstance upon the coast, which was the first part of South America to be discovered, although it might be conceivable in the far interior—especially in view of the proximity of the busy and populous city on the lake, a port of greater importance than La Guayra in some respects, full of modern life and trade. Maracaibo was at one time one of the principal educational centres of South America. Unfortunately the bar at the mouth of the harbour unfits the place for the entry of large vessels.

In this district lie the important petroleum fields, which have been made the seat of recent enterprise for the production of that coveted oil of commerce.

CHAPTER X
THE LANDS OF THE SPANISH MAIN
VENEZUELA AND GUIANA

If, as we have said, the approach to the Republic of Venezuela at La Guayra seems forbidding and inaccessible, it must not be inferred that this is an inevitable characteristic of the coast. The Caribbean Hills are splendid in their aspect from the sea. They are forbidding in their grandeur. The mighty ramparts rise almost sheer from the ocean for thousands of feet, with cloud-veils flung across them at times, and if, from the steamer's deck, we may wonder how access to the hinterland can be gained, we shall find that Nature has furnished her passes, and some of the early English adventurers of the Spanish Main scaled these, as we may read in the stirring pages of Hakluyt.[4] Personally, I retain strong impressions of these cool-appearing, towering ramparts of Nature seen whilst sweltering in the tropic heat on shipboard.

Moreover, the great spurs of the Andes die out into the sea as we go east, and so Nature has broken down the rampart, giving vent to her marvellous hydrographic forces, which here triumph over the orographic, in the Gulf of Paria and the delta of the Orinoco, clothed with the densest of tropical vegetation, the home of wild beast and wild man, as shortly we shall observe.

There are further memories of British activity in regard to Venezuelan seaports, more modern, less picturesque than those we have already remarked. For, in the year 1903, the loans and arrears upon interest, the defaulted payments and disputed interpretations of contracts, in railway construction and other matters, and alleged arbitrary behaviour on the part of Venezuelan Government officials, came to a head, with the result that Great Britain, Germany and Italy sent a combined fleet to blockade the seaports, and an enforced settlement of the creditors' claims was brought about.

However, these unfortunate incidents are of the past. Venezuela has shown a desire for more cordial relations with the outside world. Lately she sent a representative to London with the purpose of inaugurating closer commercial relations with Britain.[5]

We have now to explore the great river of Venezuela, the famous Orinoco.

The Orinoco, which pours its huge volume of water into the Atlantic on the northern shore of the continent, through a vast delta of over thirty mouths, a volume derived from over four hundred tributaries which descend from the spurs of the Andes or from the wild and mysterious forests of Guiana, flows through what might be one of the richest valleys of the earth's surface, and doubtless in the future may so become. But, like the valley of the Amazon, its resources are comparatively little utilized at present. Devastating floods, malarious forests, ferocious crocodiles are some of the elements the traveller encounters on the higher waters of this great stream, notwithstanding that Columbus wrote to his Spanish sovereign that he had "found one of the rivers flowing from the Earthly Paradise."

Unfortunately it may be said that the Spaniard and his descendants have wrought destruction rather than benefit here, and the population of the valley is less now than it was four centuries ago.

We may ascend the Orinoco, in the stern-wheel steamers which ply thereon, for about four hundred miles to Ciudad Bolivar, which town forms the chief and indeed almost the only trade centre, and in the rainy season, when the river is high, which is generally from June to November, by smaller craft up the lengthy affluents. Such are the Apure, the Meta, the Arauca and the Guaviare, many hundreds of miles in length, rising far away to the west amid the Cordillera, the cold eastern slopes of whose lofty summits condense and pour down torrents of water into an extraordinary network of rivers which flow across the plains of Colombia and Venezuela, flooding enormous areas of land in their passage to the main stream. Boats and barges may reach the Andes, whose beautiful landscape forms the water-parting of this remarkable fluvial system.

THE MAINLAND FROM TRINIDAD, AND VIEW IN THE DELTA OF THE ORINOCO.

Vol. II. To face p. 34.

In the dry season snags and sandbanks render navigation almost impossible on many of these tributaries, and in some cases in the remote districts the hordes of savages who dwell on the banks add to the dangers of the voyager. There are miles of rapids on certain of the waterways, and great cataracts, whilst the forest comes down to the water's edge, forming an impenetrable screen of tropical vegetation, in which the traveller who strays from his way is lost. This jungle is flooded in the rainy season, the waters driving back all animal life to the higher ground.

From the east comes the great Ventuari affluent, with its unexplored headwaters in Guiana.

The Orinoco River is of much interest, whether to the traveller or the hydrographer, and doubtless some day its potentialities will be more greatly utilized. In some respects this fluvial system would lend itself to the improvements of the engineer, and might perform for the region which it waters services such as the Nile renders for Egypt, instead of being, as it is, largely a destructive agent. The general slope of the river is comparatively slight, and thus canalization and consequent improvement in navigation might be carried out. Nearly a thousand miles from the mouth the waters of one of the principal affluents are little above sea-level, but the rise and fall of the flood is sometimes as much as fifty feet, and confluences two miles wide in the dry season are increased three or four times during the rains.

One of the most interesting features of these rivers, as already remarked, is found in the singular natural canal connecting the Orinoco with the Amazon—the waterway of the Casiquiare Canal,[6] which cuts across the water-parting of the two hydrographic systems. Here the adventurous canoe voyager may descend from the Orinoco and reach the Rio Negro, falling into the Amazon near Manaos.

The endless waterways of the upper reaches of the Orinoco share often that silent, deserted character which we shall remark upon the Amazon tributaries, and which indeed, is common to tropical streams often. Bird and animal life seems all to have concealed itself. Even the loathly alligator is not to be seen, nor the turtle, nor other creature of the waters. Occasionally, however, a scarlet ibis appears to break the monotony, or an eagle or heron. For mile upon mile, league upon league, there may be no opening in the green wall of the dismal forest, until, suddenly, as we pass, the wall gives way, a small clearing is seen, with perhaps a Carib Indian hut, dilapidated and solitary, whose miserable occupant, hastily entering his canoe, shoots out from the bank with some meagre objects of sale or barter in the form of provisions or other.

Such, however, is not always the nature of these rivers. The scene changes: there are sandy shores and bayous, beautiful forest flowers and gorgeous insect life, the chatter of the monkeys and the forms of the characteristic tropical fauna. Rippling streams flow from inviting woodland glades untrodden by man, and high cascades send their showers of sparkling drops amid the foliage and over the fortress-like rocks around. Wafted along by sail or paddle, guided by the expert Indian boatmen, the craft weathers all dangers, and the passenger sees pass before him a panorama of the wilds whose impression will always remain upon his mind. Thus the charm of exploration never fails, and, borne upon the bosom of some half-unknown stream, the traveller's cup of adventure may on the Orinoco be filled to the brim.

For many hundreds of miles these western tributaries of the Orinoco flow through the *llanos*, as the plains of this part of South America—in Colombia and Venezuela—are termed, whose characteristic flatness we shall remark from the deck of the vessel. A sea of grass stretches away to the horizon on every side, giving place in some districts to forest.

The level plains, lying generally about four hundred feet above the sea, were once the home of enormous herds of cattle and horses and of a hardy, intrepid race of folk known as the *llaneros*, men who kept and tended the cattle and were expert in horsemanship and woodcraft. These folk flourished best in the Colonial period. They formed some of the best fighting material in South America, and made their mark in the War of Independence, when, under Bolivar, the Spanish yoke was thrown off. Again, civil war, revolution and hardships and losses consequent thereon seriously reduced their numbers, and to-day both they and their herds have almost disappeared.

The great plains which were the scene of these former activities might, under better auspices, become an important source of food supply, both for home and foreign needs. They could again support vast herds of cattle on their grassy *campos*, irrigated by the overflow of the Orinoco. This overflow, it is true, causes extensive lagoons to form, known locally as *esteros* or *cienagas*, but these dry up in great part after the floods, which have meantime refreshed the soil and herbage.

> "The great green or brown plain of the Llanos is often beautified by small golden, white and pink flowers, and sedges and irises make up much of the small vegetation. Here and there the beautiful 'royal' palm, with its banded stem and graceful crown, the *moriche*, or one of the other kinds, forms clumps to break the monotony, and along the small streams are patches of *chaparro* bushes, cashew-nuts,

locusts and so forth. The banks of the rivers often support denser groves of ceibas, crotons, guamos, etc.; the last-named bears a pod covered with short, velvety hair, within which, around the beans (about the size of our broad beans), is a cool, juicy, very refreshing pulp, not unlike that of the young cocoa-pod. Along the banks of the streams in front of the trees are masses of reeds and semi-aquatic grasses, which effectually conceal the higher vegetation from a traveller in a canoe at water-level."[7]

Much stress has been laid upon the possible economic value of the *llanos* by some writers, whilst others regard these possibilities as exaggerated.[8] Their area is calculated at 100,000 square miles. They are neither prairies nor desert. During a large part of the year they are subject to heavy rainfall and become swamped, followed by a drought so intense that the streams dry up and the parched grass affords no pasture for stock. There is a total lack of roads, and the rivers are unbridged, and the region is far from the ocean. The trade wind blows fiercely across them.

The view over these vast plains as the traveller's eyes suddenly rest upon them as he descends the Andes is very striking, and has been described by various observers, among them Humboldt.

In the wet season, when the river overflows, the cattle are driven back to higher ground. When the waters retire alligators and water snakes bury themselves in the mud to pass the dry season.

In this connexion stories are told of travellers and others who, having camped for the night in some hut or chosen spot, are suddenly awakened by the upheaval of the ground beneath them and the emergence of some dreadful monster therefrom. A certain traveller's experience in the night was that of being awakened by the barking of his dogs, the noise of which had roused a huge alligator, which heaved up the floor of the hut, attacked the dogs and then made off.[9]

As for the old type *llanero*, half Spanish, half Indian, the wild, brave, restless, devil-may-care cowboy, a Cossack of the Colombian Steppes and a boastful Tartarin full of poetic fire rolled into one, is rapidly disappearing. Vanished is the poetry and romance of his life, if it ever really existed outside of his remarkable *cantos*, wherein heroic exploits as soldier, as hunter and as gallant lover are recounted with a superb hyperbole. He seems to have tamed down completely, in spite of the solitary, open-air life, and in spite of the continuance of a certain element of danger, battling with the elements.

Encounters with jaguars, reptiles, savage Indians are, however, the rarest of episodes in the life of even the most daring and exposed *llanero*.[10]

A "picturesque" character of original *llanero* stamp was the notorious President Castro of Venezuela, who defied the whole world at one time, and almost succeeded in bringing about a conflict between England and the United States over the Guiana-Venezuela boundary.

The wild tribes of Venezuela, and part of British Guiana, are typified in those inhabiting the delta of the Orinoco. They have preserved their racial character in marked degree here, and have been regarded as an offshoot of the Caribs.

> "They are dark copper in colour, well set up, and strong, though not as a rule tall, and with low foreheads, long and fine black hair, and the usual high cheek-bones and wide nostrils of the South American 'Indians.' Where they have not come into contact with civilization they are particularly shy and reticent, but they soon lose this character, and some are said to show considerable aptitude as workmen.
>
> "Living as they do mainly in the delta, their houses are of necessity near water, and are raised from the ground as a protection against floods, being sometimes, it is said, even placed on platforms in trees. The roof is supported in the middle by two vertical posts and a ridge pole, and is composed of palm-leaves, supported at the corners by stakes. The sides of this simple hut consist of light palm-leaf curtains, and the floor is of palm-planks. The hammocks are slung on the ridge pole, and the bows and arrows of the occupants fixed in the roof, while their household furniture, consisting of home-made earthenware pots, calabashes of various sizes, etc., lie promiscuously about the floor. Some of the Warraus are nomadic, and live in canoes, but the majority are grouped in villages of these huts, with captains responsible to the Venezuelan local government authorities.
>
> "The staple diet of these people is manioc and sago, with *chicha* (a mixture of manioc meal and water). For clothing they dispense with everything in their homes, except the *buja* or *guayuco*, a tiny apron of palm-fibre or ordinary cloth, held in position by a belt of palm-fibre or hair. That worn by women is triangular, and often ornamented with feathers or pearls. Among the whites the men always wear a long strip of blue cloth, one end of which passes round

the waist, the other over the shoulder, hanging down in front; the women have a kind of long sleeveless gown. For ornament they wear necklaces of pearls, or more frequently of red, blue and white beads, and tight bracelets and bangles of hair or *curagua* (palm-fibre); some pierce ears, nose and lower lips for the insertion of pieces of reed, feathers or berries on fête days. The characteristic dull red paint on their bodies is intended to act as a preventive against mosquitoes, and it is made by boiling the powdered bark and wood of a creeper in turtle or alligator fat. All hair is removed from the body by the simple but painful process of pulling each one out with a split reed.

"Marriage, as is usual among savage races, takes place at a very early age, the husband being often only fourteen, the wife ten or twelve years of age. Polygamy is common, but not universal; where a chief or rich man has several wives, the first, or the earliest to become a mother, takes charge of the establishment during the absence of the owner on his hunting or fishing expeditions. The girls are sometimes betrothed at the age of five or six years, living in the house of the future husband from that time on.

"At birth the mother is left in a separate house alone, where all food that she may need is placed for her, though she remains unvisited by any of her companions throughout the day; meanwhile the father remains in his hammock for several days, apparently owing to a belief that some evil may befall the child; there he receives the congratulations of the villagers, who bring him presents of the best game caught on their expeditions. This male child-bed, or *couvade*, is common to many of the Indian tribes.

"The dead are mourned with elaborate ceremony—shouting, weeping and slow, monotonous music; the nearest relatives of the defunct cut their hair. The body is placed in leaves and tied up in the hammock used by the owner during life, and then placed in a hollow tree-trunk or in his canoe. This rude coffin is then generally placed on a small support, consisting of bamboo trestles, and so left in the deserted house of the dead man."[11]

The wild animal life of this part of South America has always been of interest, whether to the scientist or the general reader. It is varied, as it is in Mexico and elsewhere in Spanish America, by the natural topographical and climatic divisions of *tierra caliente*, *tierra templada* and *tierra fria*, or hot, temperate and cold lands respectively.

The various kinds of monkeys include the spider-monkeys, the squirrel-monkeys, the marmosets, the vampires, the jaguar and puma—the former of which has been credited with living in the high branches of the trees in flood-times, to the perturbation of the monkeys, upon whose home it intrudes, chasing them to the tree-tops. In the Andes the peculiar "Speckled bear" has its abode. The manati is a native of the Orinoco, and the sloth of its forests, as also the "Ant-bear" and armadillo.

These creatures may not always be readily seen by the passing traveller, but the birds are more present, although, as elsewhere in the Tropics, their plumage is more noteworthy than their song.

> "Beautifully coloured jays, the peculiar cassiques, with their hanging nests, starlings, and the many violet, scarlet and other tanagers, with some very pretty members of the finch tribe, are all fairly abundant in Venezuela. Greenlets, some of the allied waxwings, and thrushes of various kinds, with the equally familiar wrens, are particularly abundant, nor does the cosmopolitan swallow absent himself from this part of the world. The numerous family of the American flycatchers has fifty representatives in Venezuela, and the allied ant-birds constitute one of the exceptions to the rule, in possessing a pleasant warbling note. The chatterers include some of the most notable birds of Venezuela, and we may specially notice the strange-looking umbrella-bird which extends into the Amazon territory, known from its note as the fife-bird; the variegated bell-bird, which makes a noise like the ringing of a bell; the gay manikins, whose colours include blue, crimson, orange and yellow, mingled with sober blacks, browns and greens; the nearly allied cock-of-the-rock is one of the most beautiful birds of Guayana, orange-red being the principal colour in its plumage, while its helmet-like crest adds to its grandeur; the hen is a uniform reddish-brown. The wood-hewers are more of interest from their habits than the beauty of their plumage.
>
> "The beautiful green jacamars, the puff-birds, and the bright-coloured woodpeckers are found all over Venezuela

in the forests, but their relatives the toucans are among the most peculiar of the feathered tribe. With their enormous beaks and gaudy plumage they are easily recognized when seen, and can make a terrible din if a number of them collected together are disturbed, the individual cry being short and unmelodious. Several cuckoos are found in Venezuela, some having more or less dull plumage and being rare, while others with brighter feathers are gregarious. With the trogons, however, we come to the near relatives of the beautiful quezal, all medium-sized birds, with the characteristic metallic blue or green back and yellow or red breasts. The tiny, though equally beautiful, humming-birds are common sights in the forest, but a sharp eye is needed to detect them in their rapid flight through the dim light; some of the Venezuelan forms are large, however, notably the king humming-bird of Guayana; and the crested coquettes, though smaller, are still large enough to make their golden-green plumage conspicuous. The birds which perhaps most force themselves, not by sight but by sound, upon the notice of travellers are the night-jars; the 'who are you?' is as well known in Trinidad as in Venezuela. The great wood night-jar of Guayana has a very peculiar mournful cry, particularly uncanny when heard in the moonlight. The king-fisher-like motmots have one representative in Venezuela, but the other member of the group, which includes all the preceding birds, constitute a family by itself. This is the oil-bird, or *guacharo*, famous from Humboldt's description of the cave of Caripe in which they were first found. The young birds are covered with thick masses of yellow fat, for which they are killed in large numbers by the local peasantry. They live in caves wherever they are found, and only come out to feed at dusk.

"Other birds which are sure to be observed even by the least ornithological traveller are the parrots and macaws, which fly in flocks from tree to tree of the forest, uttering their discordant cries. The macaws have blue and red or yellow plumage, but the parrots and parraquets are all wholly or mainly of a green hue. The several owls are naturally seldom seen, and, in the author's experience, rarely heard.

"There are no less than thirty-two species of falcons or eagles known from Venezuela, and of these many are particularly handsome, such as the swallow-tailed kite and the harpy eagle of Guayana. Their loathsome carrion-eating cousins, the vultures, have four representatives.

"In the rivers and caños of the lowlands there are abundant water-birds, and the identified species include a darter, two pelicans, several herons or *garzas*, the indiscriminate slaughter of which in the breeding season for egret plumes has been one of the disgraces of Venezuela, as well as storks and ibises. Among the most beautiful birds of these districts are the rosy, white or scarlet flamingoes, huge flocks of which are sometimes seen rising from the water's edge at the approach of a boat or canoe. There are also seven Venezuelan species of duck.

"The various pigeons and doves possess no very notable characteristics, and one or two of the American quails are found in the Andes. Other game-birds include the fine-crested curassows of Guayana, the nearly allied guans and the pheasant-like hoatzin. There are several rails, and the finfeet are represented. The sun bittern is very common on the Orinoco. There are members of the following groups: the trumpeters (tamed in Brazil to protect poultry), plovers, terns, petrels, grebes, and, lastly, seven species of the flightless tinamous.

"Descending lower in the scale, we come to the animals which are, or used to be, most often associated in the mind with the forests of South America. The snakes are very numerous, but only a minority are poisonous. Of the latter, the beautiful but deadly coral-snake is not very common, but a rattlesnake and the formidable 'bushmaster' are often seen. Of the non-poisonous variety the water-loving boas and *tigres* or anacondas are mainly confined to the delta and the banks of the Guayana rivers. The *cazadora* (one of the colubers) and the Brazilian wood-snake or *sipo*, with its beautiful coloration, are common; the blind or velvet snake is often found in the enclosures of dwellings.

"One of the lizards, the amphisbæna, is known in the country as the double-headed snake, and is popularly supposed to be poisonous, but there are many species of the pretty and more typical forms, especially in the dry regions, while the edible iguana is common in the forests. There are eleven species of crocodiles, of which the *caiman* infests all the larger rivers and caños. The Chelonidæ include only two land tortoises, but there are several turtles in the seas and rivers, and representatives of this family from the Gulf of Paria often figure on the menus of City companies.

"There are some six genera of frogs and toads to represent the Amphibians, and the evening croaking of the various species of the former on the Llanos is very characteristic of those regions; one, in particular, emits a sound like a human shout, and a number of them give the impression of a crowd at a football match.

"Fish abound in rivers, lakes and seas, but, considering their number, remarkably little is known about them. Some are regarded as poisonous, and others are certainly dangerous, such as the small but ferocious *caribe* of the Llano rivers, which is particularly feared by bathers, as an attack from a shoal results in numbers of severe, often fatal, wounds. The *temblador*, or electric eel, is very abundant in the western Llanos, and is as dangerous in its way as the *caribe*.

"The insects are too numerous for more than casual reference, but it may be noted that the *mosquito* of the Spaniards is a small and very annoying sandfly; the mosquito, as we know it, is, and always has been, called *zancudo de noche* by the Spanish-speaking inhabitants of Venezuela. The gorgeous butterflies and the emerald lights of the fireflies are in a measure a compensation for the discomforts caused by their relatives, but of the less attractive forms, the most interesting are the hunting ants, which swarm through houses at times devouring all refuse, and the parasol ants, which make with the leaves they carry hot-beds, as it were, for the fungus upon which they feed.

"One of the most unpleasant of the lower forms of life in the forests is the *araña mono*, or big spider of Guayana, which sometimes measures more than six inches across; it is found in the remote parts of the forest, and its bites cause severe fever. The better-known tarantula, though less dangerous, can inflict severe bites. The extremely poisonous scorpions, and the *garrapatas*, or ticks, must be seen or felt to be appreciated.

"We may leave the lower forms of life to more technical works, but the amusing 'calling-crab' deserves special mention. With his one enormous paw of pincers the male, if disturbed, will sit upon the mud or sand and apparently challenge all the world to 'come on' in a most amusing fashion."[12]

The wild people and the wild life of northern South America remind us again that the first discovered part of the continent is in some respects still the least known and most backward. The "streams flowing from the Earthly Paradise" of Columbus still traverse an Elysium for the adventurous traveller.

The coast of the Spanish Main trends now eastwards to the possession of Britain, in the Guayanas, and the beautiful Island of Trinidad, which we shall now enter upon.

Columbus, on his voyage in 1496, approaching South America, beheld three peaks rising from a beautiful island clothed with verdure. Uniting the pious custom of his time with his impression of the topography of the new land, he called the island "Trinidad," or the Trinity. Spain held it. Sir Walter Raleigh burned its capital, and finally it fell to Britain at the beginning of the nineteenth century. To-day, this land off this wild coast, under the flag of Britain, is a revelation to the traveller, who—British or other—may have forgotten its existence. Its capital, Port of Spain, is one of the most pleasing towns in the West Indies, with two cathedrals, shaded streets, tramways, government institutions and public buildings, libraries, shops, a beautiful botanical garden and other evidences of a very modern civilization and activity. The soil is rich, the climate good, the hurricanes that from time to time devastate the West Indies do not visit it. It lies almost in the mouth of the river Orinoco. Venezuela claims it as hers. I well recollect the aspect of this foothold of Britain after the wilds of South America. But its modernity does not detract from the interest of the more ancient Spanish American communities.

British Guiana, whose coast we soon approach, and its neighbours, Dutch and French Guiana, are ranged in sequence along the Atlantic front for seven hundred miles, and present topographical conditions curiously alike.

Guiana, as a geographical term, is that district lying between the water-parting of the Orinoco and the Amazon and the coast; and is almost a topographical entity, embodying part of Venezuela. It is, in a sense, an island, by reason of the union of the Orinoco and Amazon fluvial systems by the Casiquiare.

Students of Anglo-American relations will recollect that the controversy over the boundary line between British and Venezuelan territory here became the subject of contention—and almost of war—between Great Britain and the United States in 1895, by reason of the work of the wild President Castro and the unwarranted behaviour of President Cleveland of the United States—behaviour which was greatly resented by English people in South America and which has not yet been forgotten. Happily arbitration was entered upon—Britain practically being awarded what she had justly claimed.

British Guiana is one of the neglected outposts of the British Empire, the only foothold of England on the mainland of South America, a place of considerable interest, beauty and utility, but about which the good folk of Great Britain know and perhaps care little.

The British public cannot be expected to be well acquainted with all the outlying parts of the immense empire which fortune or providence has delivered over to them, but, through their statesmen, they could, if they were so minded, bring about a much more constructive and energetic policy than that which the inaccessible and old-fashioned Colonial Office and Crown Colony officials consider does duty for government and development.

The population of this land is a handful of folk of about the size of a second-rate English town, notwithstanding that the extent of the country is equal to the whole of Great Britain. Its rich littoral is watered by large rivers, rising in a little-known interior. Sugar is produced, but might be produced in quantities to satisfy the British house-wife did British folk know anything about the subject. There are enormous timber resources and valuable minerals.

INDIANS AT HOME, GUIANA.

Vol. II. To face p. 52.

But in such development comes the cry for "labour." It is the first cry of all tropical possessions. Where is labour to come from? The remedy generally proposed is that of bringing in coloured labour from other parts of the empire, coolies and others. This policy has some fatal defects. Among these the practice of bringing in hordes of coloured men without their women or families is one of the most unwise. It is unnatural to condemn these folk to live without their female partners, and if persisted in will, sooner or later, bring serious evils upon the community that practises it. The existing labour should be more carefully fostered, and if labour be imported it should be as far as possible in the form of permanent settlers, with their wives and families, the condition of whose life and surroundings should be intelligently mapped out beforehand.[13]

Guiana brings back sad memories of Sir Walter Raleigh, he who by reason of his antagonism to Spain was a popular hero, and around whose figure much romance has centred.

Partly with the object of recouping his fortune, Raleigh sailed, in 1595, to Guiana, a voyage of exploration and conquest, with the main object of finding that El Dorado which was so strong an obsession of Elizabethan times, imagined to be hidden somewhere amid the Cordillera or forests of Spanish America. His book, recounting the incidents of this voyage, *The Discoverie of Guiana*, which he published upon his return home, is one of the most thrilling adventurous narratives of the period, although it has been said that it contains much that was romance rather than fact: and incredulity marked its reception. On his second expedition, after Elizabeth's death—an expedition which was perhaps one of the saddest of forlorn hopes, whereby Raleigh hoped, trusting perhaps to a chapter of accidents, to escape from the dreadful position of disfavour and threatened execution into which he had fallen in the reign of James I—he reached Trinidad and sailed up the Orinoco, fell sick of a fever and suffered many disasters in the endeavour to carry out his undertaking to find a vast gold mine upon territory not belonging to Spain. Should he fail, or trespass upon Spanish territory, he was to be executed as a pirate, a fate which practically befell him, though he was executed under his old sentence of conspiracy.

The illustrious Raleigh—whose name some writers love to belittle—"took a pipe of tobacco a little before he went to the scaffold," for the habit of smoking tobacco—that beautiful gift of the Spanish American Indian to the Old World—had become rooted among the Elizabethan courtiers.

But to return to Guiana. The topography of this part of South America is full of interest and variety, as are the history and customs of its people, aboriginal and other, although much of the past is marked by dreadful happenings. Wars, the deeds of buccaneers, rebellions of negroes, massacre of the whites, deaths from fevers and so forth stand out from its pages.

It is a magnificent country, with grand rivers, cascades and the most wonderful mountains and scenery, which it is difficult to surpass in any part of South America. And here the traveller and the naturalist may revel in the works of Nature.

Guiana was the first part of the New World to be explored by adventurers other than the Spaniard and the Portuguese, and to this day it stands out as foreign to the rest of Spanish America. The English, the French, the Dutch fought between themselves for its territory and its colonizing and trading stations. The English sought an El Dorado, the Dutchman thought of its tobacco—which the Spaniards would not permit him to obtain from their colonies—the Frenchman took part possibly out of national pride, thinking he ought not to be left out in the partition, but his work seems to have been of a disastrous nature ever since he set foot there. The Pilgrim Fathers, before they "moored their bark on a wild New England coast," had dreams of settling here, where the warm climate and tropic possibilities seemed to hold out greater allurements than the cold coasts of the more northern continent. When Surinam, or Dutch Guiana, was exchanged for the New Netherlands and New Amsterdam—to-day New York—few Dutchmen dissented, and some English protested.

> "Like the valley of the Amazon, to which system it may be considered an offshoot, it is a land of forest and stream. The coast is generally an alluvial flat, often below high-water mark, fringed with courida (*Avicennia nitida*) on the seashore, and mangrove (*Rhizophora manglier*) on the banks

of the tidal rivers. Where it is not empoldered it is subject to the wash of the sea in front and the rising of the swamp water behind. In fact, it is a flooded country, as the name, from *wina* or *Guina* (water) seems to imply.

"The lowest land is the delta of the Orinoco, where the rising of the river often covers the whole. Coming to the north-west of British Guiana, we have a number of channels (*itabos*) forming natural waterways through swamps, navigable for canoes and small vessels. A similar series of natural canals is found in Dutch Guiana. From the Orinoco to Cayenne this alluvium is rarely above high-water mark, and is subject to great changes from currents, the only protection being the natural palisade of courida, with its fascine-like roots. On the coast of Cayenne, however, the land rises, and there are rocky islands; here the swamps come at some distance behind the shore, and between ridges and banks of sand.

"Behind this low land comes the old beach of some former age—reefs of white quartz sand, the stunted vegetation of which can only exist because the rainfall is heavy and almost continuous. This is the fringe of the great forest region which extends over the greater part of the country. Here the land rises and becomes hilly, and the rivers are obstructed by a more or less continuous series of rocks, which form rapids and prevent them running dry when the floods recede. Behind these, to the south, the hills gradually rise to mountains of 5,000 feet, and in the case of a peculiar group of sandstone castellated rocks, of which Roraima is the highest, to 8,000 feet.

"The numerous rivers bring down vegetable matter in solution, clay and fine sand suspended and great masses of floating trees and grasses. These form islands in the larger estuaries and bars at the mouths of most of the rivers; they also tinge the ocean for about fifty miles beyond the coast from green to a dirty yellow. Wind and wave break down the shore in one place and extend it in another, giving a great deal of trouble to the plantations by tearing away the dams which protect their cultivation. Every large river has its islands, which begin with sand-banks, and by means of the courida and mangrove become ultimately habitable. In the Essequebo there are several of a large extent, on which formerly were many sugar plantations, one of which remains in Wakenaam. The Corentyne and Marowyne have also fair-sized islands, but none of these has ever been settled. Off the coast of Cayenne the rocky Iles du Salut and Connetable are quite exceptional, for the coast is elsewhere a low mud-flat, sloping very gradually, and quite shallow.

"The longest river is the Essequebo, which rises in the extreme south, and like most of the larger streams, flows almost due north. It is about 600 miles in length; the Corentyne is nearly as long, and the Marowyne and Oyapok are probably about the same length. Other rivers that would be considered of great importance in Europe are seen at intervals of a few miles all along the coast. The Demerara, on which the capital of British Guiana is situated, is about the size of the Thames, and 250 miles long, and the Surinam, on the left bank of which is Paramaribo, 300. All are blocked by rapids at various distances from 50 to about 100 miles inland, up to which they are navigable for small vessels, but beyond, only for properly constructed boats that can be drawn through the falls or over portages.

"The smaller rivers, called creeks, whether they fall into the sea or into the larger streams, are very numerous; over a thousand have Indian names. Many of them are of a fair size, and the majority have dark water of the colour of weak coffee, whence the name Rio Negro has been given to several South American rivers. These take their rise in the pegass swamps, so common everywhere, and are tinged by the dead leaves of the dense growth of sedges, which prevent these bodies of water from appearing like lakes. There are, however, a few deeper swamps, where a lake-like expanse is seen in the centre, but no real lakes appear to exist anywhere. The creeks are often connected with each other by channels, called *itabos*, or, by the Venezuelans, *canos*, through which it is possible to pass for long distances without going out to sea. During the rainy season these channels are easily passable, and light canoes can be pushed through from the head of one creek to that of another, the result being that large tracts of country are easily passed. In this way the Rio Negro and Amazon can be reached from the Essequebo in one direction and the

Orinoco in another, the watersheds being ill-defined from there being no long mountain ranges.

"The higher hills and mountains are not grouped in any order. The group called the Pakaraima are the most important from their position on the boundary between British Guiana, Venezuela and Brazil, and also from the neighbourhood of Roraima giving rise to streams which feed the Orinoco, Amazon and Essequebo. This peculiar clump of red sandstone rocks forms the most interesting natural object in Guiana. Roraima is the principal, but there are others, named Kukenaam, Iwaikarima, Waiakapiapu, etc., almost equally curious and striking. All have the appearance of great stone castles, standing high above the slopes, which are covered with rare and beautiful plants, some of which are unknown elsewhere. The main characteristics of this group are due to weathering, the result being grotesque forms that stand boldly forth, together with fairy dells, waterfalls decorated with most delicate ferns and mosses and grand clumps of orchids and other flowering plants."[14]

It is not to be supposed that British Guiana has been neglected by its modern administration. A great deal has been done in draining, in reconstructing the villages, in fostering agriculture, in organizing the natives, in providing against malaria and disease by scientific methods, such as at Panama had been found so beneficial. The treatment of immigrant labour is almost paternal in some respects. Surinam is also progressing, stimulated by the example of Demerara. Cayenne, the French possession, suffers still from being a penal settlement.

The life of the coloured folk, who so largely predominate among the population, offers many problems, whose solutions will doubtless work themselves out. The people of Guiana are possibly more varied than those of any other community in the world, with representations of every race—the European and Indo-European, the African negro, the Chinese, folk from Java and Annam, together with its own native races, and the white American, with many mixed breeds.

In the views of the writer already quoted—

"Among the other points of interest there is the impress of the three nationalities upon the negro, which are very conspicuous in the women. The French negress is unlike her sister in Surinam, and she differs also from the English type in Demerara. Again, they all stand apart from the real

African and the bush negro, illustrating the possibility of the perpetuation of acquired characters and the manner in which tribal differences have been developed. 'The French,' said an old writer, 'are a civil, quick and active sort of people, given to talking, especially those of the female sex'; the Dutch have a more heavy look and wear their clothes loose and baggy, cleanliness being more conspicuous than a good fit; the English (including specially the Barbardian) are decidedly careless and slovenly, and inclined to ape the latest fashion. A Frenchman speaks of the Demerara negress as dressing up in her mistress's old gowns and wanting a style of her own; we have seen a cook going to market in an old silk dress once trimmed with lace, now smudged with soot and reeking with grease. They all have a love for finery but no taste in colour; here and there, however, a girl with a pure white dress and embroidered head-kerchief pleases the eye and proves that dress is of some importance in our estimate of these people.

"The negro man has no peculiarity in his clothes; he simply follows the European. His working dress is generally the dirty and ragged remains of what we may call his Sunday suit. He may be clean otherwise, but his covering gives us the contrary impression. There is a character about the Demerara creole, but he is not so English as the Barbadian, who is 'neither Carib nor creole, but true Barbadian born.' Loyalty to the Mother Country as well as to his own island is very conspicuous; he has followed the white man in this as well as in his language, which retains some of the obsolete words and phrases of the Stuart period, including the asseveration 'deed en fait' for 'in deed and in faith.' These national characteristics go to prove that the negro has been changed somewhat by environment, and this can be easily seen when he is compared with the African, who is represented here and there by a few of the old people who were rescued from slavers.

"The bush negro of Surinam, who ranges also through Cayenne and into Brazilian territory, is a distinct type. Made up of a number of African tribes, and probably dominated by the Coromantee, the most independent of these, he has not been much affected by his short service under the Dutch. From a physical standpoint he is a fine fellow, muscular and brawny; a good boatman and warrior, he has held his own for two centuries. Having first gained his freedom by his strong arm, he fought to retain it; the result is a man that must be respected. Possibly he learnt something from the native Indian, but he has never been very friendly, for the aborigines do not like the negro. In Demerara, and to a less extent in Surinam, Indians were formerly employed to hunt runaway slaves, and this accounts for the ill-feeling.

"We may consider the bush negro as an African savage, very slightly altered by the change from the forests of the Congo to the wilds of Guiana. Like African tribes, the communities have no bond of union, but are each under its own granman, or chief. This segregation has been the cause of much trouble in the past, for a treaty might be made with one chief which was by no means binding on the others. Their huts are low and confined, lacking any conveniences and without order. Their few arts are of African types, and their tribal marks coarse scars. Small clearings are made near their dwellings in which ground provisions enough to support their families are raised, and sometimes a little rice to sell. They also cut timber and bring it to Paramaribo for sale, with the proceeds of which they buy finery. Latterly they have been found useful to carry gold-diggers and balata-bleeders into the interior, for they are well accustomed to navigate the rapids. In Surinam the latest estimate of their number is 8,000; a few years ago they were put down as about 25,000 in all Guiana. They do not appear to increase to any extent; in fact, judging by the number of runaways who have taken to the bush in two centuries, the decrease from war and other causes must have been enormous. Their sexual relations, which are very loose, as among negroes generally, do not consist with an increase, but at the same time there is no doubt that we have here a survival of the strongest. Whether these people will ever mingle with other negroes is doubtful; at present the bush negro despises the fellow with a master or employer, and the black man of the settled portion of the colony treats him as a savage.

"In British Guiana the runaways were hunted by Indians; it followed, therefore, that no such communities of wild men were possible. The river people are largely of mixed African and Indian blood, more often perhaps with more or less of the European. They carry on the timber trade and are prominent as boat hands. Formerly, every family had its bateau or corial, but since steamers have been plying up the rivers a craft is less needed.

GEORGETOWN, BRITISH GUIANA.

Vol. II. To face p. 64.

"The coloured people are of all shades. The offspring of black and white is the mulatto, who generally partakes equally of the character of both races, but with variations. The man is coarser-looking than the woman, but as a rule he is strong and healthy; if, however, he marries a woman of his own colour the offspring are in many cases weaker than the parents. A cob is a reversion towards the negro, the child of one black parent with a mulatto, three-quarters black and hardly distinguishable. The mustee or quadroon, who is three-fourths white, and the costee or octoroon may be considered as practically white and in many cases can only be distinguished as coloured by those who know their parentage. In Guiana colour prejudice is most conspicuous among these lighter people, for they want to marry a 'higher' colour than themselves, and are considered as degrading the family when demeaning it by coming down towards the negro. A black woman will think more of her illegitimate mulatto children than of those she has borne to her negro husband. The ideal of the pure negro is the bucra—the well-to-do European;

poor whites or coloured people are in his opinion unworthy of respect. He rarely gets on well as servant to one of his own colour; quarrels and fights are common among workmen where they are under men of their own class. The negro also despises the Chinaman and East Indian, who in turn prefer to have few dealings with them. The general result is that there are not many sexual unions between the races. Now and again a respectable black man, doctor or lawyer, marries a white woman, but such unions generally bring trouble. The tendency now is for the darker coloured people to merge themselves in the black and the lighter in the white; the probable result will ultimately be to increase the distinction and reduce the present variations.

"There will almost certainly, however, always remain a coloured class, the future of whom has often been considered by travellers and anthropologists. Some have gone so far as to say that they will ultimately be the rulers of the West Indies, but there is little foundation for such an opinion. No doubt the lighter-coloured people will in time take the place of the pure whites from their greater suitability to the climate; their number will, however, probably never be great enough to make much impression. The coloured man is not so aggressive as the educated negro, who has come to the front in late years as a political agitator, and who speaks of 'the people' as being those of his own race, notwithstanding the fact that in British Guiana they are exceeded in number by the East Indians.

"The negro is prominent in the Legislature and the learned professions; he is the schoolmaster, the dispenser or sick nurse, and the lower grade clerk, but he does not succeed as a shopkeeper. The gold and diamond diggers and balata-bleeders are also black men under white superintendence. He undoubtedly fills a place which, in his absence, could only be occupied by inferior workmen of other races, and is gradually becoming a useful member of the community. As a plantation labourer he fails, mainly because he expects higher pay than estates can afford. He is capable of doing more hard work than any other tropical labourer, but he prefers a job of a few hours rather than steady, continuous work. His passions are easily roused, and when the fit is on it is useless to reason with him. After giving his employer volleys of abuse he sometimes asks a favour as if he had done nothing. Some will boast that they bear no malice, that they are open-minded, much better than some other people who will not forget an offence. Morality is largely a matter of law. 'You can't do me nothing' is a common reply when he is told that something he was doing was wrong. Many of them are well versed in the law, for crowds assemble round the magistrates' courts every day. Sometimes one will say that if he had ten dollars to pay the fine he would do something illegal; in fact, it is notorious that people who complain loudly of poverty can often pay fines of what is to them very large amounts. One day a poor woman will be begging a penny and the next paying two to five pounds in the court. Yet they have rarely anything saved, but the fines can be raised by loans and gifts from their relations and friends.

"The East Indian will certainly be the man of the future in Guiana if the immigration system is continued. Already he is ahead in British Guiana, and forms more than a third of the population of Surinam, if we include the Javanese. Though not so strong as the negro, he is more reliable, and without him there would be no Demerara or Surinam sugar. He enjoys better health in the Tropics than other races, as is easily seen by the census returns of India and the death-rates on the plantations. A great increase of population may generally be predicted where people are kind to their children, and in this the East Indian is pre-eminent. We shall say something further about him in another place, and will only here deal with his clothes. He is probably the only real tropical man who dresses to suit the climate, and he is always well dressed. With a few yards of cotton cloth he drapes himself in a manner that could only be emulated by a great artist. Any one who knows what tight-fitting European clothing means in the Tropics can appreciate the loose folds of the East Indian. Through the ages he has learnt how to dress in a graceful and picturesque manner, which, however, is practically inimitable by others. The women wear most gaudy colours, but their taste is so perfect that there is rarely anything discordant. And yet these people are hardly ever of a higher class than that of the field labourer. This natural taste in drapery and colour must have been the result of experience during long ages; that light clothing is a success is proved by the natural increase, notwithstanding war, famine and pestilence.

"The Chinese were imported as agricultural labourers, but may be considered as failures in that line, although in other respects very useful colonists. They have been condemned in other countries as undesirable, and even in British Guiana they were once stigmatized as sly rogues and thieves. Now the stigma is undeserved, for they form a trading class of considerable importance. A few have worked at the gold-diggings as well as in the forest as wood-cutters and charcoal-burners; there is also a small agricultural settlement on the Demerara River which is a picture of clean economic cultivation. They are, however, more conspicuous for their success in carrying on small country shops, where the profits are hardly sufficient to support people who are not content with a very bare living.

"The only white men ever imported as labourers were the Madeira Portuguese. Madeira was almost ruined by the vine pest about the time of the slave emancipation, and thousands of poor people came to British Guiana. For want of care during the year of seasoning many died, and the remainder were found quite unfit for field work. They were, however, useful colonists, and are now traders and in many cases well-to-do property owners. They came as paupers, but by thrift and industry went ahead, until practically every spirit-shop and corner grocery was in their hands. Only the Chinaman can compete with them, and he only does so in the villages. The Madeiran is a law-abiding citizen, but he cringes too much to the negro. The general result of the competition of the small shops is that the poorer classes get their provisions very cheap. Unfortunately, by giving way to the demands of their customers, a condition of things has arisen that no independent shopkeeper could possibly endure. However, the Madeiran has learnt to bear and forbear, and he hardly ever resents the insults and bullyings which the negress with her penny is always ready to launch upon him. He is generally looked upon as mean, and willing to stint himself to save, but this is a character which is generally wanted in the Tropics, where the tendency to thrift is always sadly lacking.

"The native Indian can hardly be reckoned as a member of the community; he is, however, useful to the traveller, the gold-digger and balata-bleeder. As a boatman, wood-cutter or huntsman, he is in his place, but his sturdy independence prevents him from becoming a reliable servant. Make him your friend and he will do anything in his power for you, but he takes orders from no one. This refers to the man of the forest whose wants are few, and when satisfied, there is no further necessity for his working. For a gun, powder or shot you may induce him to help you; when he gets these he naturally wants to be free to use them. There is, however, a class of half-civilized Indians growing up who are fairly reliable, but they do not remain in town longer than is necessary for transacting their business as carriers of timber, charcoal and cord-wood. No Indian man can endure the trammels of civilization; sometimes a buckeen, as the women are called, will take a place as house-servant, but even these are not common. Unfortunately, the men are given to rum-drinking, and laws are made for the country districts to prevent the sale to them of spirits.

"The real wild Indian is disappearing from his old haunts. Forty years ago he could be found in many of the creeks of the Demerara River where now only a few of his degenerated descendants exist. As a huntsman he must have a sort of game preserve, which is impossible where gangs of wood-cutters and balata-bleeders carry on their work. He still exists, however, in the far interior, living in much the same way as he did when America was discovered, except that he does not fight. The men are still expert hunters and fishermen, and the women as proficient in cultivating and preparing the staff of life, cassava-bread. Their old weapons, the bow and blow-pipe, are largely replaced by the gun, but the large fishes about the rapids are still shot in the old way."[15]

The things of the natural world which meet the eye of the observant traveller are of extreme variety and interest here.

"Nowhere in the world, perhaps, are such beautiful adaptations to natural conditions and such perfect interdependence. The trees bear nuts and fruits to feed monkeys, rodents, birds, bats and fishes, and because these are present in such numbers the cat family is also well represented. Again, every tree has flowers that require insect fertilization, consequently myriads of insects are here; these, in turn, are kept within bounds by ant-eaters, birds, monkeys, lizards, and those classes of insects which feed on them, such as mantids, wasps and robber flies. In the water the smaller fishes feed on fallen fruit; they provide sustenance to the larger species, which in turn become the prey of alligators and otters. On the ground, in the water, and up in the trees the struggle goes on by which the balance of life is kept even. Notwithstanding this universal war on every side, species hold their own and develop great capabilities according to their needs. Beautiful contrivances have been gained to suit the conditions under which they live, among them being protective coloration and the careful adjustment of means to the end, whether to catch and hold or to get away. The jaguar stalks the acourie so that not a twig is snapped or a leaf rustled, but the sharp rodent is always on the alert, ready to leave its feed of nuts the moment it recognizes the nearness of its foe. Under this pitch-dark canopy, through which no glimmer of moon and stars can penetrate, many a painful tragedy goes on every night. But the acourie still lives, in spite of its enemies, for, like its relation, the guinea-pig, it is very prolific. The Indian says that every animal has its tiger; he himself is one of these, and must move as silently or be content to go without meat."[16]

Guiana is within comparatively easy reach of Europe and the United States. It cannot be doubted that, in the future, it will more and more become a resort of travel, and possibly of much greater settlement and development. Its bad name will be lost: its virtues brought to the front.

South of the Guiana region and of the Orinoco lies the great region of the Amazon Valley, which we shall now traverse.

CHAPTER XI
THE AMAZON VALLEY
IN COLOMBIA, ECUADOR, VENEZUELA, BOLIVIA, PERU, BRAZIL

The River Amazon, whilst it has not the classic interest of the Nile, nevertheless appeals to the imagination in a way that that now well-mapped and travelled waterway may not—in its still mysterious and gloomy solitudes, traversing the largest areas of virgin forests on the face of the globe, spreading its vast and numberless arms over an area unexceeded in size by any other river.

The Amazon is born amid the high ranges and the snowy peaks of the Andes—the greatest mountain range in the world being a fit parent of the earth's greatest river. These high streams watered the territories where dwelt a civilization or native culture, moreover, as ancient perhaps as that of Egypt, the Andine people, and their successors the Incas of Peru, the remains of whose temples and habitations are still to be encountered on headland and plateau in those high regions of the great Cordillera, as we have already had occasion to see.

Except for a few towns upon its main stream, which were brought into being by reason principally of one natural product—the rubber of the forests—the presence of civilized mankind upon its waters or its shores is almost a negligible quantity.

The first echo of the white man's voice in the woods and across the waters of the Amazon was in the year 1540, when a party of intrepid Spaniards, after the Conquest of Peru, trusted their fortunes to its mighty bosom and floated eastwards into a world of which they had no knowledge, and, borne down by the current across an entire continent for nearly three thousand miles, were carried into the Atlantic Ocean.

The voyage is one of the most remarkable in the history of fluvial, or indeed of any navigation. Let us briefly recall it.

One day early in the above-mentioned year there was movement in the city of Quito, the ancient capital of the Shiris, in the northern kingdom of the conquered Incas, when a body of Spaniards, captained by Gonzalo Pizarro, brother of the famous Conquistador of Peru, Hernando, set forth to reach a fabled land of gold, an unknown El Dorado, which Indians, imaginative or deceptive, told their white masters lay far within the forest fastnesses beyond the Andes, a land of "Oriental spices," an empire in some beautiful and languourous region which might far surpass in riches and enjoyment anything which even Peru had yielded.

A clever guerilla captain, esteemed the best lance and master of horse in Peru, Gonzalo Pizarro, fired by the idea of this fresh conquest, called together over three hundred Spaniards, part of the retinue of the Government of Quito to which his brother had appointed him. Half the company were mounted, all were well equipped: a mountain of provisions was borne by a band of four thousand Indian servants; a great herd of swine was driven in the rear, further to furnish food for the party; and a thousand dogs, some of a ferocious breed, to hunt down Indians should such be necessary, completed the outfit. Quito lies in a broad recess of the Andes, leaving which the expedition climbed the forbidding and snow-crowned slopes which lay between them and the forests beyond, and disappeared.

Little did the members of this eager band, or the folk of Quito, know of what lay in store, or how the forces of Nature should overwhelm even so well-prepared an expedition.

The many tributaries of the River Amazon that have their rise in this portion of the Andes cut their way through extremely rugged territory, profound gorges, buried in tangled forests, where passage even for a few travellers must often be cut out through the jungle, and which to a large body of horsemen offered almost impenetrable obstacles. The intense cold and rarefied air of the mountain solitudes caused considerable suffering to the explorers, and the traveller to-day, whilst impressed with the grandeur of the scenery of the high Andes of Ecuador, crowned by the magnificent avenue of snow-capped volcanoes of which Chimborazo and Cotopaxi are the chief, gladly escapes from the inclement altitudes to the warmer climate of lower elevations. Then, as now, the land was frequently shaken and devastated by terrific earthquakes and discharges from the volcanoes, and it would appear that such a state of unrest was abroad at the moment when Gonzalo and his party appeared, as if Nature resented their intrusion.

However, at length a land known as that of Canelas, or perhaps so named by the Spaniards from the profusion of beautiful cinnamon-bearing trees, the name being Castilian for that spice, was reached. This was as far as the leader had expected to come, and finding their hopes unrealized, it would indeed have been well had the band returned to Quito, reading from the dreadful forest its true lesson. But, lured onwards by the tales of the Indians, who persisted that a few days' march beyond there lay a land teeming with gold, and inhabited by civilized and docile peoples, they pressed onward. Broad plains opened to the view, those vast savannas of the *Montaña* of the Amazon plain, and trees of stupendous growth, such as perhaps only the equinoctial regions of America produces, interspersed with beautiful flowering shrubs.

But it is a peculiarity of these regions that Nature herein provides practically nothing for the sustenance of man. Of extreme fertility under cultivation, there is little of fruits or game such as would support life, and the traveller to-day caught in these vast solitudes without an ample supply of provisions may wander about miserably, far from human aid, until he perishes. Moreover, the incessant deluges of rain which descend upon this part of America, and which are indeed the sources of the mighty flood of the Amazon, cause provisions to deteriorate and clothing to decay, and add infinitely to the burdens of the traveller. So it befel the band of Spaniards. Their provisions, after several months of travel, had become exhausted, and their clothing was reduced to rags. Part of the herd of swine had escaped, and now they were obliged to subsist on the lean bodies of the dogs and of their horses, together with such roots—often unknown and poisonous— which they dug up in the forest.

In this condition Gonzalo and his companions reached the borders of the considerable river which, known later as the Napo, is one of the principal Ecuadorian tributaries of the Amazon, and which to them, accustomed to the comparatively small rivers of Europe, seemed an enormous stream, for so far they had not gazed upon the Amazon itself. Some encouragement was derived from this river; its waters were at least a living thing; its current might be a highway leading to the desired land.

IN THE PERUVIAN MONTAÑA.

Vol. II. To face p. 78.

At a point where the Napo—after the manner of many of these Andine rivers—rushes through a narrow chasm cut like an artificial canal through the last range of the mountains to escape to the plain the band crossed, constructing a frail bridge by the method of felling a huge tree across it, over which men and horses painfully made their way, losing, however, one of their number, an unfortunate Spaniard, who, missing his footing, seized with vertigo, plunged downwards several hundred feet into the boiling torrent which thundered along the rocky gorge.

Little was gained here. There was still no prospect of the promised land. They were spent with toil and hunger; their provisions and their powers were alike exhausted. Tribes of savage Indians were occasionally met, who fought from behind rock or thicket with deadly poisoned arrows; tribes such as still exist to-day in parts of this wild region of the Amazon basin, and which still receive the traveller in similar fashion. To go on or to return—that was the question which now pressed itself on Gonzalo and his companions. But still the insidious tales of gold and plenty lured them on.

At a point where the walls of the Amazon forest closed in impenetrably upon the river verge, as is the natural character of these waterways, monotonous by reason of their enclosure of the trees and creepers, and affording no pathway along their banks, Pizarro called a halt. It was decided that the present mode of progression was impossible. They must take to the stream. A vessel of some sort must be constructed.

Necessity aiding their efforts, the Spaniards, after two months' work, built a "brigantine," a vessel rudely constructed from the timber of the forest joined together with nails from the horses' hoofs, rendered watertight with the tattered clothes of the travellers used in lieu of oakum, soaked in natural gums which abound in the trees, in the place of pitch. This craft was capable of carrying only part of the Spaniards: the remainder must continue to force their way along the shore.

And now we hear of Orellana, destined to navigate the Amazon, in this, the first European vessel—born of the forest, however, and not of any foreign seaport—to float upon its waters, the first white man to do so. For although the mouth of the Amazon had been visited by the Spanish navigator, Pinzon, some time before, in 1500, the river had only been ascended for some fifty out of its several thousand miles of navigable waterway. Orellana, the lieutenant of Gonzalo, was given command of the brigantine, which aided in transporting the weaker members of the party; and thus, floating and journeying, the expedition proceeded onwards.

But food, with the exception of "toads, serpents and a few wild fruits," now gave out entirely. The last horse had been eaten. Famine and death stared the expedition in the face. They could not go on on foot. It was necessary that the vessel should be dispatched to obtain succour from that fruitful land which it was still believed lay but a few days distant, at a point where, according to information obtained from wandering natives, the River Napo united its waters with those of the main stream of the Amazon. Orellana, with fifty of the band, was instructed therefore to descend the river and return with all speed with the much-needed assistance. He embarked, and the brigantine and its company disappeared from view round a bend of the river.

This was the last that Gonzalo and his remaining companions ever saw of the vessel. They waited for weeks, supporting themselves heaven knows how, day by day straining their eyes, hoping to see the form of the returning bark upon the waters, but all was in vain.

Meantime, Orellana and his crew, borne down by the swift current, reached in three days the point of confluence of the Napo and Amazon, a mighty flood of waters, but there was no sign of the land of promise, and instead of being able to load up with provisions and return, he could barely obtain sustenance for his ship's company; nor did it seem possible to make his way back against the current. What should he do? Were it not better to proceed on his way, descend the river to its mouth, reach the Atlantic, proceed to Spain and the Court, and cover himself with glory as the discoverer of the great Amazon and all the vast territory it traversed might contain? Eagerly his companions accepted the idea. As to those left behind they must succour themselves, and turning their prow downstream again the brigantine pursued its way, swept along for two thousand miles by the vast waters of the river.

How they escaped the dangers of rocks, whirlpools and savage Indians; how they found considerable settlements of natives, and at length reached the mouth of the river, and taking ship arrived at the Court of Spain needs not to be related here. Orellana received considerable honour at the hand of the Spanish Sovereign, with command over the territory he had discovered.

The unfortunate Gonzalo and his companions, thus left starving in the Amazon forest, suffered many vicissitudes and many lost their lives. They were forced to return to Quito without having reached any El Dorado of their dreams. The backward journey was one of the most terrible in the early history of America, and out of all that great band which set forth with such high hopes only about eighty Spaniards and half that number of Indians returned to tell the tale—little over a hundred haggard adventurers, who, falling down on the floor of the cathedral, rendered thanks to heaven for their own escape from the terrors of the Amazon wilds.

Thus ended the first expedition to the Amazon.

It was Orellana who gave the river its name. On his dangerous journey adown the current, his band fought with what they believed to be an army of women-warriors, or *Amazonas*, who rushing from the depths of the forest, attacked the white men, but who, in reality, were only wild Indians in loose cotton chemises or shirts flying in the breeze. There is no legend here of an empire of women.

That the Amazon could be navigated was again shown later by Pedro de Texeira, who, with his companions, performed the great feat of ascending from the mouth of the river up to Quito, and returning thence—a marvellous voyage for that period.

The River Napo, by which the Spaniards first entered upon the main stream of the Amazon (there was an earlier exploration of the mouth of the river in Brazil), is but one of many great navigable tributaries which traverse the territories of those nations—Ecuador, Colombia, Peru, Bolivia and Brazil—which lies partly within the region. Many thousands of miles of such navigable waterways intersect it, some of them very little known or used.

We may gain an idea of the size of the region drained by the Amazon by noting that it covers four-tenths of the entire area of South America. Yet less than a hundred square miles of it is cultivated, and its "population"—if the term may be used for the bands of savage or semi-savage Indians that dwell there and the few white settlements—number perhaps half of that of the city of London: a few million souls, who are lost in this immensity of forest, jungle and river.

The chief obstacles to travel and development in the valley are the broken or flooded nature of the country, the impenetrable forests, through which, except off the few trails, the traveller has to hack his way by means of the *machete*, wielded by his Indians. The heavy rains, the mosquitoes and the malaria, the unreliability of the natives. Dangers from wild beasts have been exaggerated. The worst of these is the mosquito! The forests are not teeming with beasts of prey, although they are to be met with. Often the traveller may pursue his way for vast distances without seeing any living creature, and he must not depend upon game for any particular addition to his larder, for there is little, in many regions. Food must be carried, and the matter of transport is one of the most serious obstacles. Without adequate supplies the traveller will starve, and leave his bones in the dismal forest, as has befallen many an adventurer here.

Except by actual travel no adequate idea of the Amazon forests can be obtained: of their alternating gloom and splendour, of their superabundant vegetation, of the impenetrable ramparts of their dense foliage and matted trunks. The forest is the largest area of virgin woodlands on the face of the globe, extending back from the Atlantic seaboard to the slopes of the Andes for more than 2,500 miles, and ranging in breadth from 200 miles on the coast, at the mouth of the river or in Brazil to 900 miles between Venezuela and Bolivia.

The marvellously rich flora is among the wonders of the world. The principal characteristic is in the variety of genera and species. A single acre of ground may contain hundreds of different species of tree and shrub, including palms, acacias, myrtles, mimosas and others. The forest is in this unlike the great coniferous or other forests, and the condition is not favourable in a commercial sense as regards the industry of timber-cutting, although industrial kinds of its trees afford the basis of profit. The trees are not always of great height here, the average being perhaps a hundred feet, with many kinds reaching two hundred feet, the shorter varieties being upon the flood-plains.

The remarkable tropical growth is shown in the myriad lianas, or creepers, which often bind the mass together, overgrowing even the tallest trees. The traveller who has had to cut his way through these networks of vegetation can best understand their impenetrability. Above his head may tower that monarch of the forest the "Cow-tree," or Massaranduba. This remarkable tree takes its name from the milk, or milky sap, it yields—a latex used in rubber-curing and for medicinal purposes. The timber is valuable for shipbuilding, and is also esteemed by railway-builders for sleepers, the wood being highly resistant, whether in air or water. Here, too, the mighty cedar rises amid its neighbours, growing to an immense height; its great trunk a hundred feet to its first branch. The wood is light, strong, and susceptible of a high polish and is valued for these qualities for many purposes.

Here is another tree we shall view with a special interest in these forest fastnesses. We shall regard it with such interest not only for its great height—for it is one of the loftiest on the Amazon—but by reason of its familiar product, as it is that which produces the Brazil nut. The tree, however, will not be crowded by its neighbours, loving the open ground. It is slender relatively for its height, perhaps three or four feet in trunk diameter. Of the two varieties one is known as the Bertholetra, the other the Sapucaya.

The collector of Brazil nuts will have a care not to approach the trees in a high wind, that is when the nuts are ripe. For the nuts, enclosed in their capsule or covering, are as hard and heavy as a small cannon-ball, and will certainly crack his crown if by mischance one falls upon his head. Prudently he waits until the pod falls, or, opening the lid with which Nature has furnished it, flings the enclosed nuts abroad, where they may be gathered. Many nuts, however, are wasted in this dispersal. The only capital required by the nut-gatherer is that involved in the ownership of a boat.

In view of the appreciation of the Brazil nut in foreign lands, and its high price, the industry of its gathering, it would be supposed, might have been more extensive.

The monarch, in a commercial sense, of the Amazon forests is the rubber, the beautiful *Hevea* and others. These have their own special habitat. They are not found anywhere, but are solitary in their nature.

For description of the animal life of the Amazon we must turn to those works of naturalists and travellers who have made this field their special study. There we may learn about the manati, or sea-cow, one of the most remarkable of mammals, growing at times to a size of twenty feet in length, having its home in the lower and larger reaches of the river. The world of the monkeys embodies fifty species. We find them up as high as the denser parts of the Peruvian Montaña, and a colony of these creatures in conclave is always a remarkable sight, with their semi-human attributes. We shall see the sloth, and hear and see the jaguar as also the peccary. The alligator will be our constant companion amid the backwaters, and a dangerous and voracious one at times he proves. The turtles may furnish the traveller with its flesh and eggs for food, as it has done for the Indians always. The traveller on occasion need not despise, moreover, the flesh of the monkey, however repugnant it may seem in life to contemplate the creature as a constituent of the forest larder. The mighty boa-constrictor will be seen by the fortunate. The brilliant plumage of the many-hued birds is perhaps a compensation of Nature for the lack of song of the many feathered tribes of the valley. As for the parasitic creatures, the ticks, the dreadful ants and a host of others, the traveller here will rarely fail to make their close acquaintance.

The western or upper edge of the Amazon Valley differs much from the denser region such as that to which the foregoing description regarding the forest applies, conditions obtaining more particularly in the Brazilian portion of the territory. This upper edge—extending, however, in some cases a long way to the east—is known in Peru as the Montaña, and embodies a much more broken and diversified landscape, more beautiful and more habitable. Bolivia, Colombia and Venezuela also partake in territory of this character, which is formed by the slopes of the Andes.

As the traveller descends the eastern slopes of the Cordillera, whose tablelands and ridges we have traversed in a previous chapter, and leaves behind him the vast grass-covered uplands, with their towering peaks, he enters upon the line of tree-life, which lies at an elevation of perhaps 11,000 feet: enters indeed upon another world. The climate becomes warmer, the mists lie heavier, thickets of flowering shrubs spread their beauty, cascades of falling water are projected like giant fountains over sheer precipices, and timber-clad ridge and profound cañon, between whose walls the torrential rivers now hurry eastwards, diversify the journey; transformation scenes which delight the eye and give an added zest to the arduous march.

A very small portion of the Montaña is occupied or inhabited. The old Inca civilization did not penetrate it, nor did the Spaniards of the Colonial period, nor yet did the white folk of the Andine Republics establish more than nominal sway over savage nature and savage man in these remote regions. Beyond the few settlers who live isolated from the world, the folk consist of more or less uncivilized tribes of Indians.

Each of these tribes generally bears its distinctive name and has its various customs—curious, useful or bestial. The Aguarunas of the Marañon build fixed dwellings and cultivate the soil. They are of middle stature, the women often well-featured, and both sexes wear short garments, in distinction to other tribes which go naked and unashamed. A warlike people, fighting with poisoned arrows, they have on various occasions destroyed the white man's settlements. These people signal their messages through the forest for long distances by means of the *tunduy*—a hollow log tautly suspended from a cord attached to a tree, and which reaches the ground, and struck hard blows with a club it emits a far-carrying sound, which, under a species of "morse" code, carries the message onward—a kind of native "wireless-telegraphy."

The Campas Indians occupy an enormous territory on the great Urubamba and Ucayali Rivers, and have assimilated some degree of civilization and are friendly to the whites. The Nahumedes are those who attacked Orellana and were taken for women-warriors. The Orejones are so called from the practice of making their ears of enormous size, by inserting weights in the lobes. The Huitoto Indians, in Peru and Colombia, were those who suffered under the excesses of the Putumayo, the great stream descending from the Colombian Andes.

It would be impossible here to enumerate the many tribes of the Montaña. Some of them were influenced by the Incas, and in consequence are of a higher calibre. The Incas, according to the legends, had a God-given mission to civilize the rude folk of Western South America, and marvellously they carried it out, in a way that puts the modern white man to shame, with his ruthless negligence or with the studied barbarity he has visited upon the poor aboriginal rubber-gatherers.

Many of these tribes cultivate the ground and subsist upon the fruits of their toil. Many of them have a more or less hazy belief in a Supreme Deity, evolved from their inner consciousness or inherited from the Incas or from the childhood of the world. The tribes have no particular cohesion, and are thus at the mercy of whoever may oppress them. At the head of each tribe is generally a *curaca*, a chief chosen by reason of his superior strength or ferocity. Often they dwell in huge community-houses.

The "Conquest of the Montaña" is for the Peruvian people a matter of considerable moment; the region, embodying what in the future may be perhaps the most valuable part of the territory of the Republic, and the Government is becoming more humanely alive to its potentialities.

It has been calculated that the aggregate length of navigable waterway of the Amazon affluents in Peru exceeds 10,000 miles, for steamers varying from a draught of twenty feet down to two or four feet; that is during high-water period throughout a part of the year. This navigability is reduced to about half the distance in the dry season.[17] In addition, the smaller channels for vast distances may be utilized for canoe-journeys.

The *Oriente*, or corresponding region in Ecuador, offers analogous conditions for navigation, although more limited in extent.[18] In Colombia, as described elsewhere, navigation is possible by small craft from the fluvial system of the Amazon to that of the Orinoco, a remarkable hydrographic condition.

UNCIVILIZED FOREST INDIANS OF THE PERUVIAN AMAZON.

Vol. II. To face p. 90.

In Bolivia the Amazon system provides also some 10,000 miles of navigation (and the Plate system a further thousand miles). The principal affluent in Bolivia of this fluvial network is the Madeira and the Mamoré.

The famous Madeira-Mamoré railway was built to avoid the cataracts and rapids on that river, and provides a link in a chain of 2,000 miles of river navigation, serving Bolivia and Brazil. The line has had a terrible history, in the deaths during earlier explorations of the route and during its construction, brought about by the adverse forces of Nature in these forest wilds.

We reach the lower terminus of this railway by the steamer which ascends the Amazon from Para and Manaos, at Porto Velho, 1,000 miles upstream from the last-named town, and here our vessel, which may have brought us from Liverpool or other European ports, lies 600 feet above the level of the sea, where it has ascended under its own steam, 2,000 miles from salt water. Here the impenetrable curtain of the forest closes in, and from it timidly emerge the harmless—if sometimes cannibal—little Indian folk who dwell in its sombre depths.

"The northern region, including the territory of Colonias, the department of El Beni, and a portion of that of La Paz, is that in which the river navigation is most considerable, for it is in this region that the majority of the *barracas* are situated. These are the establishments installed on the river banks by which the rubber of the region is collected. They are at the same time warehouses for the storing of rubber and stores containing the most varied merchandise. The *barracas* are often surrounded by plantations.

"Despite their number and their importance, the rivers of this part of the country are subject to the common fate of all the higher affluents and sub-affluents of the Amazon—namely, a considerable diminution of their waters during the dry season, which renders the channels difficult and unreliable on account of the obstacles which accumulate at certain points. It is really only during the season of high water that steam navigation is easy and rapid; in general, on the Rios Beni and Madre de Dios, the steamboats run freely from December to May. From June and July the steamers encounter increasing numbers of obstacles and are exposed to the risk of a sudden fall of water, when the types of vessel peculiar to each river come into use, particularly from August to November.

"During the months of July and August navigation is inconvenient on account of the expanse of mud, which has not as yet had time to harden, but is left uncovered by the falling waters on either bank, making landing a difficult matter. The reefs uncovered at low water and the entanglements of tree trunks disappear with the rise of the waters, and the steamers recommence running.

"Descending the rivers during high water, navigation is both easy and rapid, but it is also rather dangerous on account of the swiftness of the current. It is difficult to estimate the time needed to navigate this or that river, as the day's journey, ascending or descending, varies according to the river, the amount of water in it, the kind of vessel employed, the amount of cargo carried, and the crew which steers or propels the vessel.

"The vessels peculiar to the rivers of those regions which do not permit of steam navigation, and which are everywhere employed when the waters are low, are the *balsa* and the *callapo*, each a species of raft; together with boats of various dimensions—*monterias* or *batelon*, *egariteas*, *canoas* or *pirogues*, the latter being dug-out canoes.

"The *balsa* is a raft consisting of seven pieces or trunks of a peculiar and very light wood known as *palo de balsa* (raft-wood); these pieces are either bound together or pinned with stakes of *chonta*, a kind of black palm which is very hard. The fore part of the raft is narrowed slightly, and the trunks are arranged on a curve whose elevation is perhaps eighteen inches, so that the sides are higher than the middle. Each of the seven trunks is perhaps five inches in diameter. On the framework thus made is placed a platform of plaited bamboos, known as *chairo*; this platform, which is intended for the reception of the cargo, and on which any passengers take their places, is called the *huaracha*. At each end of the raft a space of three to five feet is left free of any covering; here sit or stand the three boatmen who form the crew—two at the bow and one at the stern. A good raft is usually twenty-two to twenty-six feet long, by five to six feet wide, and will carry about 7 1/2 cwt. of cargo, as well as the three boatmen.

"A *callapo* or *monteria* consists of two or three *balsas* lashed together; such a raft will carry as much as 34 cwt. The crews of these rafts, according to their dimensions, consist of three to fifteen men; these men are Leco Indians, or Mosetenes, or Yuracares, who are highly skilled in this kind of navigation.

"The pilot is the captain of the crew; he is naturally the calmest and the most expert; the *punteros*, who are stationed at the two ends, are the strongest; the rest are the rowers. The navigation of the *balsa* is terribly hard work when mounting against a current; as a rule two men go ashore and tow the raft from the bank, pulling on a rope some fifteen yards in length; a third, armed with a pole sixteen or eighteen feet long, keeps the raft a certain distance from the bank, so that it shall not run aground. Where the water is too shallow to float the raft, it must be dragged over the stones in the bed of the river. In reaches where it is impossible to make one's way along the bank the raft is poled up-stream, a method of progression which costs more effort and is less speedy.

"The crew of a *balsa* or *monteria* will usually navigate for some ten or twelve hours a day, during which they will perhaps make nine or ten miles; to rest, eat or sleep they go ashore, which action is known as *encostar*.

"The navigation of the Mapiri (one of those rivers which run into the Beni) must be made in *balsas* or *callapos* manned by Leco Indians. From Mapiri the descent is rapid as far as Huanay, and the only obstacles are a few sunken reefs, which cause dangerous vortices in the impetuous stream. Where the Mapiri takes the name of Kaka (river of rocks)—that is, at the confluence of the Coroico—there are many dangerous passages full of surface rocks. This river finally flows into the Beni.

"The Rio Boopi also leads to the Beni; rafts like those of the Mapiri are piloted by Mosetenes Indians. The passage is rapid, for at the outset the river enters a narrow gorge, that of the Meniqui, in which the current flows at a dizzy speed; eventually the Beni is reached at Guachi. Rafts are employed as far as Rurenabaque and Salinas or Puerto Brais, as between the two ports there is the dangerous passage of the Altamirani, which is encumbered with rocks and rapids.

"The Rio Beni is then freely navigable by large steamers as far as Riberalta, at the mouth of the Madre de Dios, a distance of 473 miles. Steamers cannot proceed to Villa Bella on account of the Esperanza rapids or falls, which are 340 yards long with a declivity of 18 feet; the river here is nearly a thousand yards wide, and its depth is three fathoms. The current is so rapid that boats and rafts must be unloaded both ascending and descending. The railway now being built between Riberalta and Guayaramirim will circumvent this difficulty.

"The Rio Madre de Dios, on the banks of which there are numerous settlements, is navigable for steamers during the months of high water from Riberalta as far as its remotest tributaries, such as the Inambari, the Manu, the Tambopata or Pando, etc.; during the rest of the year the journey must be made in *callapos*. The navigation of this river is difficult only about the middle of its course, where there are two rapids, which are, however, completely covered when the water is high. The Madre de Dios is navigable by its affluents as far as the outlying spurs of the Andes.

"To pass from this river to the Rio Acre there is a choice of two routes. One may go overland from the Carmen *barraca* to Cobija, or by water, by way of the Rios Manuripi and Tahuamanu, affluents of the Orton. The Orton, an affluent of the Beni, is, like the Madre de Dios, navigated by steam-launches during the season of high water, and by other vessels—rafts and canoes—all the year. Numerous *barracas* (rubber stations) lie along the Orton, whence one can easily pass to the Rio Acre."[19]

The wealth of the rubber-bearing regions of Peru and Bolivia has of late years been made the subject of considerable study, but the industry of rubber-gathering and export has been overshadowed from a variety of causes. The Acre territory in Bolivia and that of Colonias have been regarded as regions of untold wealth in this respect. Difficult roads lead thereto from the capital of the Republic, but these, in some cases, are extremely picturesque.

INDIANS OF THE NAPO, PERUVIAN AMAZON REGION.

Vol. II. To face p. 96.

"Hardly has one crossed the Cordillera when on all sides, on the flanks of the mountains, far off on the plains, in the valleys, the vast virgin forests show as great sombre patches emerging from fields of verdure. Varied as the vegetation which composes them, some seem impenetrable, their huge trees garlanded with lianas and loaded with innumerable parasites. These trees are not of great diameter because, being huddled so closely together, they struggle upward to seek the air and the light.

"Others, undulating in the wind, waving their palmated crests, seem like the parks of some destroyed Eden; they are often so burdened with flowers that when the wind blows it is as though the snow were falling. Some of these forests are incessantly alive with myriads of splendidly coloured birds and monkeys of every species; others, on the contrary, are so full of silence and shadow and mysterious solitude that the traveller might believe himself in a virgin world.

"Everywhere innumerable watercourses drain the country; some contain flakes of gold, but the true wealth of the country is in its vegetation, so marvellously vigorous and varied that even in America the forests of the Amazonian basin are proverbial.

"Although this region lies wholly within the Tropics, it contains every plant and animal to be found under the sun—from the cedar to the banana with its velvet leaves, which never thrives but under the Equator; from the jaguar to the heat-loving monkey gambolling in the sun, and even, in the great plains of the east, from the shepherd watching his flocks to the collector of rubber and the planter of cocoa established beside the rivers or in the depths of the odorous valleys.

"Despite these natural advantages, the greatest to be found on earth, civilized man inhabits this region only at rare and isolated points. This portion of Bolivia is still a wilderness almost unknown, into which the Bolivians of the high plateau, attracted and held by the metalliferous strata from which they strive to tear their treasure, only come by chance to tempt fortune by the exploitation of rubber. As men are everywhere prone to generalize, the territory of Colonias has the reputation of being full of mosquitoes, Indians and wild beasts, each category more dangerous than the other. There is a manifest exaggeration here. Certainly the mosquitoes are an objectionable race, but they are not found everywhere, and as for the Indians, if they have on occasion displayed a certain malevolence— possibly justified, but of which they themselves are always the first victims—they are as a rule invaluable as boatmen and collectors of rubber, and it is regrettable that they are not more numerous. Remain the dangerous wild beasts: well, they fear man far more than he fears them, and moreover they speedily desert such localities as man inhabits or frequents.

"The climate of the territory of Colonias varies according to the proximity of the chain of the Andes, the altitude, the abundance of watercourses, and the direction of the winds. The temperature in May, June and July is mild and agreeable, moderately cool in the morning and evening, varying between 53·6° and 76·6° from 6 p.m. to 6 a.m., and from 76·6° to 89·6° between 10 a.m. and 4 p.m. during the hottest months (September to December). Rarely does the thermometer rise or fall above these extremes. The normal temperature does, however, suffer a sudden fall when the cold south winds blow that are known as *surazos*; they come in September and produce violent storms with great and almost daily variations in the temperature, which may give rise to affections of the lungs and throat as the sequel to sudden chills. The force and direction of the winds contribute greatly to modify the salubrity of any region; places reputed to be unhealthy have become notably healthy when the forest has been opened or closed in a given direction.

"The great defect of the climate here is the abundance of the rains. They fall continually through the whole rainy season, which lasts from December to May. The vapours of the Atlantic are brought up by the east winds, which are prevalent at this season; on reaching the Cordillera they are chilled as the air expands and loses heat with its increasing altitude; then the vapours condense and fall in torrents of rain, which often lasts for whole days together. But these rains are never cold, so they are not unpleasant as such rains would be in Europe; one braves them without thinking anything of it, as in Europe one braves a summer shower.

"When it does not rain (the dry season lasts from June to November) the climate is delightful; the middle of the day is hot, with a somewhat heavy heat, although the sky is usually covered with a diaphanous mist which tempers the rays of the sun.

"Floods are caused not only by rains in the western mountain regions, but also by local rains. They are dependent on the slope of the surface and the insignificant fall of the rivers. When the larger rivers are full the tributaries rise because their waters are dammed up or even flow backwards. The waters then become stagnant in every sense of the word, and decompose rapidly through the action of the heat and the vegetable and other detritus which they contain; at such times they produce paludian fevers; principally in April and May, when the waters begin to fall and the larger rivers receive the supplies of stagnant waters released from their tributaries. As the fall continues the mud left uncovered on the banks becomes an additional cause of fevers.

"These paludian fevers, which are prevalent more especially during the rainy season, attack more particularly the rubber collectors—an ignorant and primitive population who know nothing of the most elementary rules of hygiene. Careless or imprudent whites pay the same penalty.

"The lack of medical attendance, intemperance, negligence which results in the drinking of stagnant water drawn from pools or swamps or from the river banks; above all, the bites of the mosquito, against which no protection is employed, and which convey malaria to healthy but debilitated persons: these are the causes of the ravages occasioned by paludism in this region, as throughout the Amazon basin.

"These conditions do not obtain throughout the Territory; there are numerous healthy localities as, for example, along the middle reaches of the Madre de Dios, in all parts which lie at any altitude, and in regions not subject to floods where a portion of the forest has been cleared in order to give the beneficent breezes a free course. On the other hand, and we speak from long personal experience, any healthy individual of robust or even average constitution can maintain himself in good health, suffering, in the long run, from nothing worse than a little anæmia, by observing the following rules:

"Do not drink stagnant water unless it has been boiled; if one must drink unboiled water take it from the river, not from the bank, but from the middle of the current; do not walk or ride or exert yourself in the morning fasting; cover the loins with a belt of wool or flannel; take short but frequent baths or douches in order to facilitate perspiration and to avoid congestion of the pores; and in fever belts, or during the rainy season, take daily, as a preventive, four to eight grains of sulphate or hydrochlorate of quinine (in a cachet or compressed in tabloids) as well as a few granules of arsenic; finally, keep to an abundant and nourishing diet and do not forget that the nights being cool it is indispensable to take warm clothing and good blankets; and, most important of all, never omit the protection of mosquito-nets.

> "Such is the territory of Colonias and the greater portion of El Beni, a land of magnificent vegetation; it is regarded, not without reason, as a country where tropical agriculture may have a future before it. At present this vast country possesses a population of only some 40,000 to 45,000 inhabitants, without counting its 15,000 to 18,000 wild Indians, a population of which the greater portion if not the whole is occupied in the production and transport of rubber, the chief product of the territory and the neighbouring countries."[20]

The conditions of life and the treatment of the rubber gatherers of the Amazon Valley were brought strongly before the world some years ago by the disclosures of the Putumayo, in Peru, when it was shown that terrible ill-treatment was meted out to the aborigines of the forests, in the greed for rubber. They were shown to be frequently starved, flogged to death, or tortured in various ways, their "crime" being that they would not or could not bring a sufficient quota of rubber. A powerful London company was involved in these scandals, but the directors, when brought before a Parliamentary Commission, protested that they had no knowledge of the matter.

It cannot be doubted that cruelties are still practised on the Indian folk, in the rubber-districts of Peru and Bolivia, under the curtain of the forest, although the authorities of these countries have taken measures to endeavour to prevent these.

The condition of the rubber industry in the Amazon forests are not, of course, all barbarous or uneconomic. It afforded, or affords, a means of livelihood to a considerable number of people, and created wealth where there was little other means of enrichment. It is, to an extreme, unfortunate that the industry is, in parts, a dying one—superseded in large measure by the active rubber plantations of the Straits Settlement, Malaysia and elsewhere. But it remains to be seen if, some day, under better auspices, the Amazon industry will not be revived. It also remains to be seen if the exotic plantations of Malaysia will be permanent, or whether exhaustion of the soil and other matters with what is an exotic industry there may not lead to deterioration, or decrease of the commodity and its yield, although it is to be hoped that such eventualities may not occur.

It is affirmed by experts that wild rubber is superior to plantation rubber. One of the evils of the Malaysian system is that whereby coolie labour is brought in without their women, and consequently no family life is possible among these coloured workers. In the Amazon Valley there are no such restrictions, and under better auspices the native rubber-gatherer could prosper and multiply. Herein lie important matters for the future, especially for that fortunate part of civilized mankind that rides on the rubber tyres of the modern motor-car.

Let us cast a passing glance at a rubber metropolis, here on this mighty South American river, at Manaos, a name familiar at least to the London reader of financial newspapers and to the shareholders of British concerns thereat—for British capital furnishes light, and power, and docks, and other matters, for some of these Amazon river ports.

Near that fork of the great river where on the one hand the black waters of the Rio Negro come down from a thousand miles' course from Venezuelan, Colombian and Ecuadorian forests and mingle with the muddy waters borne from the Peruvian Marañon and its tributaries, there stood, in the middle of last century, a riverside village of Indians, a handful of Portuguese, negroes and half-breeds. From this humble beginning a city sprang to being, the geographical and trade centre of the Amazon, with every comfort and every vice of modern civilization. What was the cause of this transformation? It was the discovery of the uses of rubber, the exploitation of the "black gold" of the forests. Manaos grew until the place, to which all the rubber-producing lands of the neighbouring Republics are tributary, provided ninety per cent. of the world's supply of rubber. It has not, however, given its name to this commodity, which has been associated rather with that of Para, another riverside city near the mouth of the Amazon, itself created largely by this trade.

"Formerly the basin of the Amazon was almost unpopulated. In 1848 the city of Belem, the only one in Amazonia, had 15,000 inhabitants, but two years later an epidemic of yellow fever greatly diminished their number. As for Manaos, even thirty years later it was only a village; Mathews, who visited it in 1879, estimated its population at 5,000. The Indian tribes of the forest refused to work; and a few thousand half-breeds, *tapuyoz*, a mixture of Portuguese, Indian and negro blood—were utterly inadequate to draw upon the wealth that men were beginning to recognize in the bordering forests. Labourers were demanded on every hand. The first immigrants, who settled about Manaos, were Indians from Bolivia and Peru; but their numbers were wholly insufficient.

"It was the influx of the inhabitants of Ceará, during the draught of 1877-79, that made the development of the rubber trade possible. From that date the colonization of the forest proceeded rapidly. The seekers of rubber dispersed themselves throughout Amazonia; but the region most regularly exploited was the basin of the Rio Purus and that of the Rio Jurua. These two rivers are navigable for a greater distance upstream than any other of the affluents of the Amazon, and in the virgin forest, which the rubber-seekers were the first to invade, the exportation of rubber is only possible along the navigable water-ways. The Brazilians who mounted the Purus and the Jurua did not stop at the Bolivian frontier; a war with Bolivia very nearly broke out on the subject of these lands, which a few years earlier had not even been explored. The foundation of the independent Republic of Acré, the treaty of Petropolis, and the cession of Acré to Brazil, were the result of the westerly march of the rubber-seekers.

"The economic development of Amazonia was prodigiously rapid. In 1890 it exported 16,000 tons of rubber; in 1900, 28,000 tons; in 1905, 33,000 tons. It became, next to San Paulo, the most important centre of exportation in Brazil.[21] The cities increased in size; the population of Para surpassed 100,000; that of Manaos attained to 50,000; and this growth of the cities, which was more rapid than the growth of the total population, is an index to the rapidity of the commercial development of the country. The Amazon became one of the great river highways of the world, serving not only the Brazilian Amazon, but also the regions of Peru which are crossed by the upper tributaries, and a portion of Venezuela, where products descend to Manaos by the Rio Negro.

"The exportation of rubber created wealth on all sides. All other occupations were abandoned for the collection of rubber. The herds of cattle on Marajo and the cocoa plantations along the banks were neglected. Similarly, in the neighbouring districts of Guiana the fields and plantations were abandoned on the discovery of 'placer' gold. No one thought of anything but rubber. Up to that time the country had produced its own food; now it had to resort to importation. It became a market in which the other States of Brazil were able to sell their products at a highly profitable rate. All these changes were due to the importation of labour from Ceará."[22]

We have seen elsewhere that the ocean steamer which carries us up the Amazon will reach the Peruvian port of Iquitos, a place of much importance, due to its position in the very heart of the continent, the centre of a vast tributary region, whose value the future will better be able to estimate.

A region of the utmost interest lies before the traveller who will adventure himself upon these tributary streams and the diversified territories which they drain. There might be fleets of motor-boats upon these waterways, whether bent upon pleasurable exploration, whether upon business and trade. The civilized folk of the eastern slopes of the great Cordillera are, metaphorically, stretching out their arms towards the east, casting eager glances thereover, for from thence must come economic prosperity and civilized peoples.

And now, once more, a glance at the past in the great valley, though brief, at those influences which have tried to make for good as against evil: the forces of the Church and the missionary.

The Jesuit friars in Brazil have had terrible charges laid at their doors, but they and the Franciscan friars did noble work in the forests and the rivers among the savage or humble denizens. Had their work been allowed to continue, it might have flourished greatly. Among the missionaries the name of the Padre Samuel Fritz stands out (as did that of Las Casas in the Cordillera and the coast). Fritz gave the greater part of his life, from 1686, in work among these unfortunate Indians. But the fighting between the Spaniards and the Portuguese, around the forts built near Manaos, destroyed this work. The Portuguese dispatched armed bands against the Spaniards, and destroyed the missions and the settlements, waging war in their jealous pretensions over this savage territory.

It will be recollected by students of history that the Popes—among them Paul III—strove to protect the Indians of the Amazon. This Pontiff, in 1537, issued a decree to the effect that "the Indians were men like others." Later, alarmed by the atrocities which were perpetrated in Mexico and Peru upon the aborigines, the Pope sanctioned slavery as a means of avoiding such horrors. In 1639 Pope Urban VIII excommunicated the captors and vendors of Indians, but later the Portuguese Government allowed the establishment of slavery. Under Dom John VI, the Indians were to be considered as "orphans" in the eyes of the law, and to be protected. But the present condition of the Amazon Indians is one in which they appear to have no civil or legal rights.

As regards modern missionary work here, this is full of difficulty, for if it is to be carried out by Protestants it involves a clashing with the Roman Catholic priesthood, which naturally occupies the whole continent. The work, however, whether by Protestant or Catholic, is not by any means neglected, although much greater effort is needful. Such effort should go hand in hand with economic elevation—also a difficult problem, due, in part, to the attitude of vested interests in the field.

It would but weary us to dwell upon the economic possibilities of the Amazon Valley in detail. Its climate and the fertility of its soil would render possible the cultivation of all those tropical products which are needful to the growing and hungry world, which, complaining that the cost of life is unbearable, is yet unable to set its hands to the fuller development of the great fallow areas, among which lies the vast Amazon territory. Here, then, is work for the future.

We now turn to the huge Republic of Brazil, mistress of the greater part of Amazonia, and of much else.

CHAPTER XII
BRAZIL

When, in the year 1502, the early Portuguese navigators entered the Bay of Rio de Janeiro—it was the first of January, hence the name they gave to what they believed to be the estuary of a great river—they little dreamed of that superb city which, as the centuries rolled on, should arise on the edge of the sparkling waters, with their background of picturesque mountains, with a harbour perhaps the finest in the New World.

But such is the capital of Brazil to-day, and the traveller approaching Rio de Janeiro revels—if the weather be propitious—in the sunlit sea, the emerald islets that stud its bosom, the palm-fringed shores and colour of the vegetation upon the mountain slopes, fit setting for the handsome buildings, esplanades and avenues which unfold to the view. Here the beauty of the Tropics, shorn by modern science of much of its lurking dangers, combines with the handiwork of man to form a metropolis which South America may contemplate with pardonable pride as an instance of its civilization. In this vast oval bay, which stretches inland for twenty-five miles, the navies of the world might lie at anchor, and indeed the flags of all maritime nations unfurl their colours near the quays of this vast mercantile seaport below the Equator.

It is a vast land which we thus approach. Brazil spreads like a giant across its continent. Its arms are flung westwards over South America for over two thousand miles to the base of the Andes, and from above the Equator to beyond the Tropic of Capricorn, crowding its smaller neighbours—if crowding be possible here—into the extremities of the continent, an area in which the countries of Europe might be more than contained, and which is larger than the vast Anglo-American Republic, the United States.

Still almost unknown are great portions of this great territory, still inhabited by tribes as savage as when first the white man set foot upon it, or as when the faithless Orellana, Pizarro's lieutenant, abandoning his companions in the heart of the dreadful forests of the Amazon, floated down the mighty waters of that river from the source to the sea.

Brazil is, of course, not a Spanish American country, although it was at one period under the dominion of Spain; and it stands apart from the remainder of the great sisterhood of the Latin American Republics by reason of its Portuguese origin and language, although the common Iberian ancestry renders it similar thereto in other respects. It differs, furthermore, in the constitution of its people, in that the African negro race has been so considerably absorbed into the twenty-two million souls which form the population of the Republic: an admixture which is of considerable ethnological interest, and may have some important bearing on the future relation of the white and coloured races of the world.

THE BAY OF RIO DE JANEIRO.

Vol. II. To face p. 112.

The magnificent but somewhat incoherent land as is Brazil to-day, offered at the time of its discovery few attractions to the sovereigns of a Mother Country into whose coffers the wealth of Africa and of India flowed. Its poor and barbarous tribes had no stores of gold ready to the hand of the *Conquistador*; there was no civilized empire with a polity and architecture and organized social life, with armies to protect it, such as Mexico and Peru offered, and consequently neither glory nor riches urged the European discoverer or invader to tempt its hinterland and people its valleys and seaboard. For thirty years the Portuguese sovereigns paid little heed to this newly acquired dominion, except that they fought off the encroaching Spaniard and the adventurers of France, who would have entered or traded with it.

Twenty years before the Conquest of Mexico it was that the first explorer sailed the Brazilian coast—and only eight years after Columbus had sighted the American mainland—that the Spaniard, Vicente Yañez Pinzon, a companion of Columbus, with whom sailed Amerigo Vespucci—who gave his name to America—sighted the shore of what is now Brazil, near Cape San Augustine, reconnoitring the mouth of the Amazon and coasting along to the Orinoco. He took away some gems from the Indians, some drugs and a load of dye-wood.

From this later commodity of the dye-wood, the great dominion of Brazil took its name. "Brazil" was originally a legendary island in the Atlantic, which long retained its imaginary position in the lore of the forecastle and upon the ancient charts, and from this circumstance the name came to be bestowed upon that enormous part of South America which produced the red dye-woods similar to those which bore the name of Brazil in the Middle Ages.

A few months after the keel of Pinzon had furrowed these unknown seas, another explorer, Cabral, close upon Easter in 1499 (O.S.), following the course of Vasco de Gama to the east, was drifted by an adverse gale so far from his proper track that he reached this same coast, and, anchoring in Porto Seguro, erected an altar there, celebrated Mass, set up a stone cross and took possession of the country for the King of Portugal. He, like Columbus, thought he had reached India, and sent a vessel to Lisbon with the news.

Let us turn for a space to examine the great land thus brought to knowledge by these early voyagers.

To-day, the traveller in Brazil will soon be impressed by the immensity of its spaces, will remark how broad are these wide tablelands, how interminable the *serras* and mountain ranges, how boundless the forests. The territory of this great land is fifteen times that of France. It is larger than the United States (without Alaska); it is over 2,600 miles long upon the Atlantic, and 2,700 miles wide from its coast to where, across the heart of the continent, it touches the frontier of Peru. Its boundaries touch those of every South American nation except Chile. Persistent trespassers were the Portuguese in the early Colonial period, and their land-hunger carried them beyond those boundaries which the Pope, as we have seen in a former chapter, fixed between Portugal and Spain.

What is the general nature of this great territory? Here is a coastline with many sandy beaches, mangrove swamps and lagoons, with inland channels following the coast for long distances, but giving place to rolling, fertile coastal plains terminating in headlands overlooking the Atlantic waves. The coast is indented with many land-locked bays, forming large and easily accessible harbours, with others smaller and difficult of approach.

Back from this characteristic littoral, from Cape San Roque—nearly the easternmost point of South America, whose tropic headland here juts out far towards Europe—and southward to Rio de la Plata extends a vast tableland, covering half Brazil, and beyond this we reach immense undulating plains of sandy soil, forming the great depression of South America from the basin of the Amazon in the north to the basin of the Paraná River in the south.

Thus do we remark a singular incoherence and lack of symmetry in the physiography of Brazil, largely due to geological conditions. Yet Brazil is a land which has been immune from violent geological disturbances from an early time. Such oscillations as there have been have not brought to being enormous mountain chains or intensive foldings of the rocks, such as are so marked elsewhere in South America. Flat bedding or low angles mark the geological horizons since the Devonian Age, and since that age it would seem that none of Brazil has been beneath the sea. There are eruptive rocks in the Devonian and carboniferous beds, but since the Palæozoic epoch it does not appear that there has been any volcanic activity. These devastating forces of Nature seem to have had their vent on the western side of the continent. The Palæozoic beds of the interior are of red sandstones, and these have their place in marked degree in the economics and appearance of the landscape.

The formation of the country has been interestingly described by a well-informed recent writer, whom we may quote here.

> "The high plains of the interior, which shed their waters both north and south, have never been of economic importance; the valley of the Amazon has been developed only of late years, and its population is as yet small. It is therefore the tableland of the Atlantic seaboard, from Uruguay to Ceará, that constitutes the soil of historic Brazil. Through its length of 1,800 to 2,200 miles this tableland presents the greatest variety of aspect, and has no hydrographic unity. Its height is greater to the south, where it reaches some 3,200 feet. This general slope from south to north is revealed by the course of the San Francisco. In Brazil the name of Borburema is employed to denote the northern portion of the plateau. This old geographical term deserves preservation, as it represents a region which has its own peculiar characteristics. The dry season there is a long one, and the Borburema does little to feed the small seaboard rivers which flow fan-wise into the Atlantic; for the plateau in that region slopes gently to the sea.
>
> "It is otherwise in southern Brazil. From the State of San Paolo southwards the seaward face of the plateau is a huge bank, some 2,500 or 3,000 feet in height, which separates a narrow strip of coast from the basin of the great rivers inland. This long bank or watershed bears successively the titles of Serra do Mar and Serra Geral. From San Paolo to the Rio Grande no river pierces its barrier; but the streams which rise upon its landward side, almost within sight of the sea, cross the whole width of the plateau before they

join the Paraná or the Uruguay. Thus the Serra do Mar is not really a mountain range; though it has, from the sea, all the appearance of one, owing to its denticulated ridge; but the traveller who reaches the crest by crossing the inland plateau arrives at the highest point by the ascent of imperceptible gradients, and only discovers the *serra* when he breaks suddenly upon the sight of the ocean thousands of feet below.

"Beyond the *serra* is the territory of Minas; a confused mass of mountainous groups, among which it is no easy matter to trace one's way, either on the map or on the trail itself. An enormous backbone of granite, the Mantiqueira, crosses the southern portion of Minas; and the railway painfully ascends its grassy slopes. The Mantiqueira, which receives on its southern flank the rains brought by the ocean winds, is the highest point of the plateau, and the hydrographic centre of Brazil. It gives birth to the Rio Grande, the principal arm of the Paraná.

"As soon as we cross the southern frontier of the State of San Paolo the plateau is transformed; there is no more granite, and the landscape grows tamer. The primitive measures of gneiss and granite, out of which the Serra do Mar is carved, are covered to the westward by a bed of sedimentary rocks, of which the strata, dipping toward the west, plunge one after the other under other more recent strata. They consist exclusively of red and grey sandstone, and the sandy soil which results from their decomposition covers the western portions of the four southern States. The topography of the country changes with the geologic structure. The outcrops of sandstone, which one crosses in travelling westward, cut the tableland into successive flats. Irregular ranges turn their abrupter slopes towards the east, as the banks of the Meuse and Moselle in the basin of the Seine; the rivers flow close underneath them, running through narrow gorges. Even the least experienced eye could never mistake these cliffs of sandstone for ridges of granite; these are not mountain chains, not *serras*, but, according to the local term, *serrinhas*.

"In Santa Catharina and Rio Grande enormous eruptions of basaltic rocks have covered a portion of the plateau. The basalt has even reached the seaboard, and southward of the island on which Desterro is built it overlies the granites of the Serra do Mar. The south flank of the plateau, which overlooks the prairies of Rio Grande, is also basaltic. The popular judgment has gone astray, having given the same name—the Serra Geral—to the granitic chain and to the edge of the basaltic overflow, as if one were a continuation of the other.

"If we except the prairies of Rio Grande, where the pampas of the Argentine and of Uruguay commence, there is nothing in front of the Serra do Mar but a narrow sandy waste. The rains which scar the face of the *serra*, wearing it into ravines, do not irrigate it sufficiently; and the rivers, of little volume, are spent in slowly filling the marshes that border the coast; they are lost finally among the granite islets, in the deep bays which the first explorers insisted were great estuaries. From the Rio Grande to Espirito Santo the Parahyba is the only river that has been able to deposit, at the foot of the *serra*, and around its outlets, a solid and fertile alluvial plain; it is there that the sugar-mills of Campos are established.

"It is the vegetation above all that gives the various regions of Brazil their peculiar character. It is a mistake to suppose that Brazil is entirely covered with forests. The forests are concentrated upon two regions: the basin of the Amazon and a long strip of seaboard along the Atlantic coast between Espiritu Santo and Rio Grande. The forests require abundant rains; and the Serra do Mar, receiving the humidity of the ocean winds upon its dripping flanks, incessantly hidden by mists, produces far to the south the conditions which have made the Amazonian basin the home of the equatorial forest. For a distance of 1,200 miles those who have landed at the various practicable inlets have found everywhere on the slopes of the *serra* the same splendid and impenetrable forest. Even to-day it is almost untouched. It encircles and embraces Rio; it seems to refuse it room for growth, as in the tale of Daudet's, in which the forest reconquered in a single springtide the land which the intrepid colonists had stolen from it in order to found their settlement.

"Beyond the belt of swamps which extends along the coast, where ill-nourished trees, overladen with parasites, struggle against imperfect drainage and poverty of soil, at the very foot of the *serra*, the true forest begins. The dome-like summits of the great trees, ranged in ascending ranks upon the slope, completely screen the soil they spring from, thus giving the peculiar illusion that this wonderful vegetation rises, from a common level, to the extreme height of the range. Here and there only emerges from the foliage the smooth water-worn side of a granite bluff. The railway track runs between walls of verdure; the underwoods, which elsewhere suffer from the lack of light, grow eagerly along the sides of the trench-like clearing. Lianas, ferns, bamboos, grow vigorously as high as the tree-tops. One seems actually to see the brutal struggle of the plants toward the sunlight and the air. Many travellers have spoken of the sense of conflict and of violence produced by the virgin forest. There is, indeed, along the clearings cut by man, and over the trees which he fells but does not remove, a fierce battle between species and species, individual and individual; a desperate struggle for space and air. As always, it is man who introduces disorder into the heart of Nature. Far from his track order reigns, established by the victory of the strongest; and the forest which has never been violated gives a profound impression of peace and calm.

"The *serra* is the true home of the equatorial forest. But it covers beyond the ridge the southern and western portions of the State of Minas and the basins of the Rio Doce and the Parahyba. The Martiqueira very nearly marks the limit of the forests; beyond commences a dense growth of bush. I remember a long journey along the northern slope of the range upon which is built the new capital of the State of Minas, the city of Bello Horizonte. Towards the north we could see vast stretches of uncovered land; the mountains were partly clothed with narrow belts of forest, which climbed upward through the valleys to the very sources of the streams; we passed alternately through thickets of thorn and prairies where the soil was studded with the nests of termites. The dense trees, deprived of their leaves by months of drought, were beginning to revive, and were decking themselves with flowers, of a startling wealth of colour unknown to the forests of the humid regions. There it was that the bush commenced. It stretched unbroken to the north— unbroken save for the streams, which were full or empty according to the rain they had received.

"In San Paolo also and Paraná the region of afforestation is not limited by the ridge of the *serra*. Forests and prairies alternate on the plateau. The fires which the Indians used to light in the savannahs have destroyed the forest in places; yet man has played but a little part in the present distribution of vegetation. The forest has persisted wherever the natural conditions were favourable, holding tenaciously to the humid slopes of the hills or to rich and fertile soils. Certain soils, either by reason of their richness or their moisture, particularly favour the forest, while on lighter soils the trees can ill resist the drought. The diabasic soils of San Paolo are always covered with a mantle of forest; so much so that a map of the forests would be equivalent to a geological map.

"The forest of the plateau, intersected as it is by stretches of prairie, is less dense and less exuberant than the forest the *serra*; and as we approach the south the difference is yet more evident. Towards the boundaries of San Paolo and Paraná the tropical trees are replaced by resinous varieties. The immense pines of the Paraná, with straight trunks and wide, flattened crests, whose shape is rather reminiscent of that of a candelabrum with seven branches, cover with their sombre grey the wooded portions of the plateau from the Paranápanema to beyond the Uruguay. With their open foliage, pervious to the light, these woods resemble the pinewoods of Europe.

"To find the tropical forest once more we must push as far as the Serra Geral, whose southern slopes run down towards the prairies of Rio Grande, as on the east they descend towards the sea. There, on the basaltic flanks of the *serra*, is a last fragment of the tropical woods. In magnificence it almost equals the forests of Rio or of Santos. It is the equatorial forest that makes the continuity of the *serra*, not its geological constitution. When the Brazilians speak of the *serra* they think of the forest rather than of the mountains. Incautious cartographers, who have worked from second-hand data, which they have not always interpreted correctly, have sown the map of Rio Grande with a large number of imaginary ranges. One seeks them in vain when traversing the country; but one finds, in their place, the forests which the inhabitants call *serras*; the term for mountain has become, by the latent logic of language, the term for forest. Nothing could better emphasize the importance of vegetation in the Brazilian landscape; it effaces all other characteristics.

"Forest, bush and prairie change their aspect with the cycle of the seasons. The whole interior of Brazil knows the alteration of two well-defined seasons. The temperature is equal all the year through; there is no hot season, no cold season, but a dry season and a rainy season; this latter corresponds with the southern summer. At the first rains, which fall in September or October, the wearied vegetation abruptly awakens. Then comes the time of plenty, when earth affords the herds of cattle an abundant pasturage. March brings back the drought to the scorching soil. The region of rainy summers includes all the State of San Paolo, extending sometimes as far as Paraná. Further south the rhythm of vegetable life is no longer swayed by the distribution of the rains, but by the variations of the temperature, which grow always greater as one travels south. From June to September frosts are frequent in Rio Grande. The cattle on its pastures suffer from cold as much as from hunger. Spring returns, and the grass grows as the sun regains its power. This is the only portion of Brazil in which the words winter and summer are understood as they are in Europe.

"But the *ocean* side of the *serra* knows no seasons; all the months of the year are alike; all bring with them an almost equal rainfall. There vegetation is truly evergreen, everlasting, unresting. The ridge of the *serra* divides two different countries. If it is true that the division of the year into well-marked seasons, that powerful aid to the agriculturist, is the privilege of the temperate regions, then tropical Brazil is found only at the foot of the *serra* and on its slopes; the interior is another Brazil.

"Its advent into Brazilian history dates very far back. The first colonists immediately climbed the *serra*, and so discovered the vast territories which offered them a climate more favourable to their efforts. The belt of seaboard was too narrow and too hot to be the cradle of a nation. Colonization was effected otherwise than in the United States. In North America the pioneers settled along the seaboard, in a bracing, healthy climate, and there dwelt for a long period without any thought of crossing to the west of the mountains which limited their outlook. They prospered and multiplied in their narrow domain, and, having formed a nation, only then began to extend their territories toward the west. In Brazil, although the administrative capital of the colony remained upon the coast, men quickly began to penetrate the interior. To-day even to the seaward of the plateau to which the immigrants made their way, and which they have everywhere opened up for exploitation by labour, the soil remains but sparsely populated. While the forests of the interior gradually recede before the agriculturist, Brazil has kept the forest of the littoral intact, and man has not disputed the claim of the woods. They form, between the seaboard cities and the agricultural regions of the plateau, an uninhabited frontier, a sumptuous but deceptive frontage. Many travellers know nothing of the country but the seaboard forest. It deceives them as to the nature of Brazil, and as to its economic progress. The living members of Brazil are hidden behind it as behind a screen.

"After the first astonishment has abated, and when one has travelled far and for long periods, the eyes at last become tired; they become inured to the opulent scenery, and even find the landscape monotonous. The sombre green of forest or prairie everywhere hides the rocks; the soil stripped bare by the roads, is of a dull, uniform red; even the dust is red. Bright colours and broken lines are equally rare. One travels continually among rounded hillocks of green; the humid climate hides or softens the contour of hill and valley alike. The memories of one's journey's blend and grow confused; reminiscences of forests, skirted or traversed; clumps of banana-palms near fordable streams; windings of the twisted trail in the midst of undulating prairies."[23]

From mountain slopes and forest glades let us turn to glance into the Brazilian home, at the Brazilian people.

In one sense, Brazil is an old country, as far as any American nation may be termed so, and in its three hundred years of life since the white man became established within its shores life has taken on a settled form and engrafted itself upon its environment. It is a land of marked social customs and distinctions. It has an aristocracy, a culture refined and stable.

Education, music, poetry, the arts, are revered and enjoyed, and in this sense the traveller is transported to the Old World. Yet Brazil is democratic in its ideas, as far as democracy has been possible in the Latin American Republics—a matter which is of circumscribed limits at present.

The foreigner, unless he specially lay himself out to know the folk of the Latin American lands, cannot readily look into their homes. They are a people, as elsewhere remarked, full of reserve, almost mediaeval in their seclusion, sensitive, yet extremely hospitable and open-handed whenever these barriers of reserve are penetrated. This is naturally but the Iberian social character transplanted to America.

It is to be recollected, moreover, that Brazil was a slave-owning land, with all in social life that that condition brings. Brazil was always a viceregal or monarchical country too. The fall of slavery in 1888 in part brought about the fall of the empire. Thus we have here everywhere—except in the southern States where recent immigration has brought other thoughts and customs—a rigid ruling class and caste, the privileges of an old society, such as does not exist in its neighbour of Argentina, for example, and which is foreign to the United States. Essentially an agricultural country, the land, moreover, belongs almost in its entirety to this ruling class.

Yet this condition of land-owning seclusion and reserve is not necessarily accepted as a final and irrevocable circumstance. "In the cities, and especially Rio, where social life is more developed and the national character tempered by contact with foreigners of all nationalities, the country magnates, ignorant of the ephemeral passage of the fashions, are the subject of ready ridicule. The country magnate's name is never pronounced without exciting merriment."[24]

This is a curious circumstance, and shows how custom differs in varying lands. In England, for example, the "country magnate" is generally a personage upholding all that is best in the community.

In Brazil there is a marked taste for country life, such as is scarcely yet developed in the Spanish American Republics. The elegant suburb does not necessarily attract the newly rich Brazilian, who loves to return to the *fazenda*, or country estate. It has been said, however, that this is less the result of delight in rural amenities than in the lust of power, for in the *fazenda* he is absolute master, with a power over his dependants stronger perhaps than in any other land.

PALM AVENUE, RIO DE JANEIRO.

Says the writer before quoted: "One of the qualities of the *fazendeiro*, one which I ought particularly to mention, is his extreme hospitality. In cordiality, delicacy and unfailing tact the hospitality of the Brazilian surpasses the imagination of the most hospitable of Europeans. The *fazendeiro* will make every possible effort to render his house agreeable to you; if you wish to take the air the best horse is at your service; or the safest, according to your talents as a horseman; the eldest son of the house will be your companion. After dinner the family will search among the gramophone discs for the latest music, the latest French songs. In the morning, upon your departure, your host, cutting short your thanks, will assure you of the gratitude he owes you for your visit. I have witnessed this scene a score of times, and each time—whether or not I owed such fortune to my French nationality—I felt that I was received as an old family friend.

"Such hospitality introduces one to the heart of many families. These families, too, are large; ten children are considered in no way extraordinary. Paternal authority is respected; the son, upon his entrance, kisses his father's hand. The wife is occupied with household cares; the husband's duty is to do the honours of the house. A stranger rarely sees Brazilian women, except as the guest of a Brazilian family. The women do not receive male callers; for them, or so it seems to me, mundane life ceases upon marriage.[25] They marry, I believe, very young, and are absolutely under the marital thumb. Outside their family their independent life is extremely limited. Admirable mothers, one knows them rather by their children than personally; they seem to cherish their domestic obscurity. The traveller who lands in the United States is immediately surrounded, questioned, advised and chaperoned by the American woman; there is nothing of this sort in Brazil.

"In addition to its social authority, this Brazilian aristocracy enjoys political power as well. Brazil has, it is true, established universal suffrage; but the sovereign people, before delegating its sovereignty to its representatives, confides to the ruling class the duty of supervising its electoral functions. The large landed proprietors choose the candidates, and their instructions are usually obeyed. They form the structure, the framework, of all party politics; they are its strength, its very life; it is they who govern and administer Brazil. And the administration is a great power in Brazil. Its province is very wide, and much is expected from it; whether the explanation is to be found in Latin atavism, or in the material conditions of life in this limitless territory, or in the fact that the individual is so powerless, and association so difficult. It is only a slight exaggeration to say that the administration plays the same part in Brazil as in a European colony like Algeria, or as in India.

"Between the members of the all-powerful administration who during my travels granted me facilities, and their friends and relations, whose hospitality I enjoyed in their *fazendas*, I was perhaps in danger of becoming exclusively acquainted with the superior social class of which a portion directs the agricultural exploitation of the country while the remaining portion governs it. It would be a great mistake to suppose that this class, by itself, is Brazil. I have done my best to see beyond it, and to keep in mind the populace, which is both more numerous and more diversified; a confused mass of people upon whom, before all else, the whole future of Brazil depends. It lives under a benign climate; or at least under a climate which makes impossible what we call poverty in Europe. It is also a rural class; all the agricultural labour of the country is performed by its hands.

"In Southern Brazil the population has been renewed, all through the second half of the nineteenth century, by a stream of European immigration. In San Paolo the Italians have provided the long-established Paulista population with the labour necessary to the extensive production of coffee. They live on the plantations, in villages which are veritable cities of labourers. Nothing ties them to the soil; they do not seem to feel the appetite for land; very few buy real estate. They bind themselves only by yearly contracts; they readily change their employers after each harvest. No more nomadic people could be imagined; they change incessantly from *fazenda* to *fazenda*. Neither is there anything to retain them in the State of San Paolo; and not the least danger of the coffee crisis is the exodus which it is producing among the Italian colonists.

"Farther south, from Paraná to Rio Grande, immigration has resulted in the settlement of a very different population: a small peasant democracy, composed of Poles, Germans and Venetians. Being proprietors, they are firmly rooted to the soil. Just as the influx of Italians to San Paolo was not a spontaneous movement, but the work of the Paulista administration, so the German and Polish colonization of the south was evoked and subsidized by the Government of Brazil and the interested provinces. The newcomers were sent into regions hitherto unpopulated, where commercial communications could not be established and economic vitality was unknown. There they lived abandoned to themselves, without neighbours, without customers. The political and artificial origin of these colonies condemned them to isolation; isolation kept them faithful to their national customs and languages, which they would soon have abandoned under other circumstances."[26]

It is seen that the Brazilian has a strong leaning towards the exercise of the intellectual gifts of mankind. They are philosophical. The love of scientific and learned titles is strong. The doctorate—of laws, literature, medicine, science—has been a coveted distinction, indeed has been carried out to become a weakness or failing, a passion, as among all Latin American communities. At one time the ambition of every family capable of affording a superior education to its sons was that the boy should be a priest. That passed, and then he was to be a doctor, in one of the professions, and, moreover, to marry the daughter of a neighbour who was also a member of the learned class. Nearly all professions, it is to be recollected, in the Latin communities carry the doctorate with them. Nearly all statesmen are doctors—when they are not military men, and then the sword is apt to oust the diploma!

A COLONY, RIO GRANDE.

Vol. II. To face p. 132.

Now Brazil—and the same has taken place in Chile—has abolished the doctorate as being "undemocratic," has abolished the universities and all their ceremonies and the cap and gown, regarding them as too aristocratic-seeming, and, in their place, a simple certificate of knowledge is given from the "professional school."

This may seem destructive, but perhaps there is a measure of wisdom in it, for apart from a measure of danger in too marked social distinctions, the system tended among the youth of the country towards too great an aspiration for academic honours, and not enough towards the more practical and productive walks of life.

The aristocratic society of Brazil naturally centred around the monarch, for, as we have not forgotten, Brazil was the only self-contained empire in the New World, except for Mexico's short-lived monarchical regime. We may not here trespass much upon the field of history, but we shall recollect that, in 1808, the fugitive Portuguese Court, under the regent, Dom Joâo VI, sought Rio de Janeiro as his refuge. This advent gave a stimulus to the growth of the capital, which was opened to foreign commerce with the removal of industrial restrictions, printing was introduced and medicine and literature established. In 1822 Brazil declared its independence, with Dom Pedro I as its emperor. The expulsion of royalty in 1889, by a military revolt, was accomplished without bloodshed, but under subsequent presidents revolution reared its head.

Brazil is a land that has depended largely for its prosperity upon the system of what may be termed "monoculture," that is, the exploitation of one principal crop or product. In earlier times this was sugar; more recently it has been coffee. This policy, whilst it had advantages, and, indeed, may have been inevitable, has also serious disadvantages. Such products are bound for foreign markets and susceptible to the rise and fall of exchange. The producers may be enriched or impoverished by such fluctuations.

Moreover, "monoculture," as pointed out elsewhere, tends to the sacrifice or neglect of other interests, those of smaller and more varied industries, which go to make up the life of a nation, to increase its happiness, prosperity, knowledge—indeed, to feed it and supply it. There is a tendency to draw off labour under monocultural systems from smaller occupations, from local food supply and local industry, to herd labour into barracks or congested places, to discourage individual initiative and peasant proprietorship, concentrating industry into too few hands. This condition is of easy growth in such countries as Spanish America, where raw materials, rather than finished articles, are produced.

There are evidences, however, that Brazilian Governments are awakening to these matters and encouraging the implantation of a wider variety of industry. Along such paths undoubtedly lies greater national prosperity and stability.

The high protective tariffs of the Latin American countries at the same time tend to raise enormously the price of imported articles and to foster the industries of the countries themselves. In Brazil the national manufacturing industries have grown very considerable under this system of economic fostering. None is more striking than the cotton-weaving industry, and we are already in sight of the time when the country will cease to import English or other foreign cotton goods, except perhaps certain special kinds. This, of course, is sound economics (however unpleasing it may be for

British manufacturers). Brewing and soap-making are other industries that have similarly prospered in the Republic. But, so far, factories are few, comparatively, though there is some useful decentralization of manufacture. One finds tiny factories in small struggling villages where their presence might have been unsuspected, industries brought about by the immensity of distance, the high cost of carriage, which soon exceeds the value of the finished product, and thus Nature has here provided a sort of natural protective zone; factories being established where customers exist, and for the purpose of serving them, rather than for the object of sale beyond their borders. Each small factory has its own circle of customers, under these circumstances, and can rely upon its market close at hand. It enjoys a monopoly of its peculiar region.

Apart from any defects to which such a system may give rise, this may be regarded as a valuable condition, and, if preserved, may avoid in Brazil the serious evils which in some European countries, such as England, over-centralization of manufacture has given rise—a philosophy to which, however, English people have not yet awakened.

Similar conditions exist as regards agriculture: the dispersal or decentralization of industry is necessarily accompanied by the dispersal or decentralization of agriculture. Food products are grown where they are to be consumed. Each hamlet, and indeed each family, has its own fields of maize, manioc and often sugar-cane. The village is enabled not only to provide itself with employment and with manufactured articles, but with foodstuffs, and, in the future, this circumstance might give rise to an intensive general settlement and contentment.

For trading conditions it may have its adverse side. But the question is how far trading should be encouraged as against economic settlement.

"As a result of the difficulty of communications, and also, perhaps, of the defective organization of trade, Brazil is far from forming a national market. Her territory may be decomposed into a host of little isolated markets, each independent of the other, each sufficing to itself. If the prices vary, neither rise nor fall affects the outer world. In Rio I find the sugar-planters in a state of joyful excitement: in a few months the price of sugar has risen by 100 per cent. Two days later I land in Paraná; there, in the narrow tropical belt of seaboard, are a few sugar-plantations, whose crop is sold on the plateau; not in the shape of sugar, but as 'brandy,' *aguardiente*, or, strictly speaking, rum. The local crop of cane is abundant, the owners of the sugar-mills at the foot of the *serra* are grumbling at having to sell their spirit at far below its usual price.[27] Similarly the price of coffee will fall in San Paolo and in Santos, until the Paulist coffee industry appears in actual danger, and the State undertakes the perilous business of running up the prices to save the planters. Yet in Ceará there are only a few growers, who can barely supply the consumers of the State, who are selling an inferior coffee at double the usual prices, and know no other anxiety than the fear that the drought may threaten their crops. Such contrasts are frequent. If such is the case with luxuries like sugar and coffee, what of the heavier products, whose transport is still more costly?

"The limitation of the markets renders the economic life of the country unequal and ill-adjusted. It exposes it to continual partial crises which naturally check its development. When production exceeds consumption the local market cannot unload itself upon the neighbouring markets, in which the producers would perhaps receive better prices, since these, on account of the cost of transport, are shut off, as it were, by water-tight compartments. Prices accordingly fall, without any possible remedy; immediately production is limited and becomes insufficient; then prices rise, and there is no importations from without to limit their rise. Reawakened by better prices, production is once more stimulated; and its very improvement provokes a new crisis. I found the settlers of Paraná accustomed and even resigned to the sudden leaps of the market, which they had come to regard as a normal and inevitable state of affairs. They live, therefore, always in a state of uncertainty, never able to foresee what will be their resources for the coming year. The spirit of saving has decayed among them. In the same way wholesale trade used to suffer formerly from the extravagant variations of exchange. The Brazilians have at last come to understand the dangers of such conditions. There is only one remedy: to improve the means of communication. The great question of Brazil is above all a question of roads."[28]

In Brazil the question of means of transport is a serious one. The magnificent network of railways (largely built by British capital) serves only the more settled part of the country.

The great export trade of Brazil, with its staple products, furnishes a stream of gold, which, more or less, becomes dispersed throughout the country, and creates strong ties of union between the various States, which otherwise might not exist in unison.

As to sugar, however, Brazil is in large degree its own customer. The great export is coffee, as it was once sugar, and in part rubber. Meat also finds its principal market at home. Brazil will soon supply its own wants in flour, which now comes in part from Argentina.

The rise of the coffee-growing industry in Southern Brazil, in the rich State of San Paolo, has in it the element of an economic romance.

The condition was the result of Nature's geological work here. It was discovered about the year 1885 that Nature had disposed large areas of what came to be called "red earth"—a certain diabasic soil of rich decomposed lavas—in this part of Brazil, and that the coffee-shrub flourished wonderfully upon them. A coffee-planting "fever" was the result. Rich and poor flocked in to take up these lands and plant the berry; other forms of agriculture were despised; all hunted for the red-earth deposits, built their homes, set out rows of young shrubs. The forests receded, cut down by the axe of the new settlers. Towns sprang to being as if by magic, where people were drawn from the four quarters of the globe, from every nation. *Fazendas* rapidly spread, railways were multiplied, coffee occupied all minds. They thought it the one thing on earth. Coffee was their art, literature, religion.

Thus the great and to-day rich and handsome city of San Paolo grew up, into which coffee pours, to have its final outlet for the market beyond the sea, at Santos—once a dreadful and fever-stricken port, whose very name was anathema to the traveller, now a fine and fairly healthy seaport of vast importance.

A VIEW IN SAO PAULO.

The life and circumstances of the immigrants or "colonists," as they are termed, in these coffee-growing districts of Brazil is one of peculiar interest for the student of race matters and human geography, of great value in the science of colonization. Here is an account by a careful observer:

> "Each *fazenda* constitutes a little isolated world, which is all but self-sufficient, and from which the colonists rarely issue; the life is laborious. The coffee is planted in long regular lines in the red soil, abundantly watered by the rains, on which a constant struggle must be maintained against the invasion of the noxious weeds. The weeding of the plantation is really the chief labour of the colonist. It is repeated six times a year. Directly after the harvest, if you ride on horseback along the lines of shrubs, which begin, as early as September, to show signs of their brilliant flowering season, you will find the colonists, men and women, leaning on their hoes, while the sun, already hot, is drying behind them the heaps of weeds they have uprooted.
>
> "Each family is given as many trees as it can look after; the number varies with the size of the family. Large families will tend as many as eight or ten thousand trees; while a single worker cannot manage much more than two thousand.
>
> "Like the vine, coffee requires a large number of labourers in proportion to the area under cultivation; it supports a relatively dense population. The two thousand trees which

one colonist will receive will not cover, as a matter of fact, more than five to seven acres; yet the coffee supports other labourers who work on the *fazenda*, in addition to the labourers proper, or colonists. Pruning, for instance, which so far is not universally practised, is never done by the colonists, but by gangs of practised workmen, who travel about the State and hire themselves for the task. The colonist is only a labourer; if he were allowed to prune the shrubs he would kill them. Heaven knows, the pruners to whom the task is confided ill-treat the trees sufficiently already! They use pruning-hook and axe with a brutality that makes one shudder.

"When the coffee ripens, towards the end of June, the picking of the crop commences. Sometimes, in a good year, the crop is not all picked until November. The great advantage enjoyed by San Paolo, to which it owes its rank as a coffee-producing country, is that the whole crop arrives at maturity almost at the same moment. The crop may thus be harvested in its entirety at one picking; the harvester may pick all the berries upon each tree at once, instead of selecting the ripe berries, and making two or three harvests, as is necessary in Costa Rica or Guatemala. This entails a great reduction in the cost of production and of labour. San Paolo owes this advantage to the climate, which is not quite tropical, and to the sequence of well-defined seasons and their effect upon the vegetation.

"At the time of picking the colonists are gathered into gangs. They confine themselves to loading the berries on carts, which other labourers drive to the *fazenda*; there the coffee is soaked, husked, dried and selected, and then dispatched to Santos, the great export market. All these operations the colonists perform under the supervision of the manager of the *fazenda*. A bell announces the hour for going to work; another the hour of rest; another the end of the day; the labourers have no illusions of independence. In the morning the gangs scatter through the plantation; in the evening they gradually collect on the paths of the *fazenda*, and go home in family groups, tired after the day's work, saving of words, saluting one another by gestures. On Sunday work is interrupted; games are arranged; parties are made up to play *mora*, or Italian card games, with *denari* and *bastoni*. Women hold interminable palavers. Sometimes, on an indifferent nag, borrowed at second or third hand from a neighbour, the colonist will ride as far as the nearest town, to see his relations, exercise his tongue, and pit himself against such hazards of fortune as the world outside the *fazenda* may offer.

"What are the annual earnings of the agricultural worker? The conditions vary in different localities, but we may estimate that the colonist receives about 60 or 80 milreis— £4 to £5 7s. at the present rate of exchange—per 1,000 stems of coffee. This is a certain resource; a sort of fixed minimum wage. To this we must add the price of several days' labour at about 2 milreis, or 2s. 8d. A still more irregular element in the profits of a colonist's family is the amount it receives for the harvest. By consulting the books of several *fazendas* I was able to realize the extent of this irregularity. Sometimes the wage paid for the harvest is insignificant, while sometimes it is greater by itself than all the other sources of income put together. It is calculated at so much per measure of berries given in by the colonist. When the branches are heavily laden, not only is the total quantity greater, but the labour is performed more rapidly, and each day is more productive. Years of good harvest are for the colonist, as for the planter, years of plenty. With this important element essentially variable, how can we estimate the annual earnings of the colonist?

"His expenses, again, cannot be estimated with any exactitude. An economic family will reduce them to practically nothing, if it has the good fortune to escape all sickness, and so dispense with the doctor, the chemist and the priest.

"What really enables the colonists to make both ends meet is the crops they have the right to raise on their own account, sometimes on allotments reserved for the purpose set apart from the coffee, and sometimes between the rows of the coffee-trees. They often think more of the clauses in their contract which relate to these crops than to those which determine their wages in currency. A planter told me that he had learned that a party of colonists intended to leave him after the harvest. We met some of them on the road, and I questioned them. 'Is it true that you are engaged to work on Senhor B———'s *fazenda* for the coming year?'—'Yes.'—'What reason have you for changing your *fazenda*? Will you be better paid there? Don't you get over £6 a thousand trees here?'—'Yes.'—'How much do they offer you over there?'—'Only £4.'—'Then why do you go?'—'Because there we can plant our maize among the coffee.'

"The culture of coffee is thus combined with that of alimentary crops. Almost all the world over the important industrial crops have to make room in the neighbourhood for food crops. Every agricultural country is forced to produce, at any rate to some extent, its own food, and to live upon itself if it wishes to live at all. In Brazil the dispersion of food crops is extreme, on account of the difficulties of transport; it is hardly less in San Paolo, in spite of the development of the railway system. Each *fazenda* is a little food-producing centre, the chief crops being maize, manioc and black beans, of which the national dish, the *feijoade*, is made.

"It even happens at times that the colonists produce more maize than they consume. They can then sell a few sacks at the nearest market, and add the price to their other resources. In this way crops which are in theory destined solely for their nourishment take on a different aspect from their point of view, yielding them, a revenue which is not always to be despised.

"The colonists make their purchases in the nearest town, or, more often, if the *fazenda* is of any importance, there is a shop or store—what the Brazilians call a *negocio*—in the neighbourhood of the colonists' houses. Its inventory would defy enumeration; it sells at the same time cotton prints and cooking-salt, agricultural implements and petroleum. An examination of the stock will show one just what the little economic unit called a *fazenda* really is. Although the colonists are to-day almost always free to make their purchases where they please, the trade of shopkeeper on a *fazenda* is still extremely profitable. He enjoys a virtual monopoly; the *fazendeiro* sees that no competitor sets up shop in the neighbourhood. The shop is the planter's property; he lets it, and usually at a high rent, which represents not only the value of the premises, but also the commercial privilege which goes with it. It is a sort of indirect commercial tariff levied by the planter on the colonists; a sign of the ever so slightly feudal quality of the organization of property in San Paolo. The custom that used to obtain, of the planter himself keeping shop for the profit, or rather at the expense of his colonists, has generally disappeared.

"One of the most serious of the planter's anxieties is the maintenance of the internal discipline of the *fazenda*. This is a task demanding ability and energy. One must not be too ready to accuse the planters of governing as absolute sovereigns. I myself have never observed any abuse of power on their part, nor have I seen unjustifiable fines imposed. The *fazendeiro* has a double task to perform. He employs his authority not only to ensure regularity in the work accomplished, but also to maintain peace and order among the heterogeneous population over which he rules. He plays the part of a policeman. The public police service cannot ensure the respect of civil law, of the person or of property. How could the police intervene on the plantation, which is neither village nor commune, but a private estate? It falls to the planter to see that the rights of all are protected. Many colonists have a preference for plantations on which the discipline is severe; they are sure of finding justice then. The severity of the planter is not always to the detriment of the colonist.

"Individually the colonists are often turbulent and sometimes violent; collectively they have hitherto shown a remarkable docility. On some *fazendas*, however, there have been labour troubles, and actual strikes; but they have always been abortive. The strikes have not lasted, and have never spread. One of the means by which the planters maintain their authority and prevent the colonists from becoming conscious of their strength is the prohibition of all societies or associations. They have had little trouble in making this prohibition respected. Among an uneducated group of labourers, of various tongues and nationalities, the spirit of combination does not exist. We have seen the development of working-men's societies, of socialistic tendencies, in the cities of San Paolo, but nowhere in the country. An incoherent immigrant population, but lightly attached to the land, is not a favourable soil for the growth of a party with a socialistic platform. One must not look for agricultural trade unions in San Paolo. The contract between the planter and his labourers is never a collective but always an individual contract.

"Accounts are settled every two months. It often happens, even to-day, that the colonist is in the planter's debt. The planter has kept up the custom of making advances, and every family newly established in the country is, as a general rule, in debt. But the advances are always small, the colonist possessing so little in the way of securities; he has few animals and next to nothing in the way of furniture. His indebtedness towards the planter is not enough, as it used to be, to tie him down to the plantation; that many of them continue to leave by stealth is due to their desire to save their few personal possessions, which the planter might seize to cover his advances. At the last payment of the year all the colonists are free; their contract comes to an end after the harvest. Proletarians, whom nothing binds to the soil on which they have dwelt for a year, they do not resume their contracts if they have heard of more advantageous conditions elsewhere, or if their adventurous temperament urges them to try their luck farther on.

"The end of the harvest sees a general migration of the agricultural labourers. The colonists are true nomads. All the planters live in constant dread of seeing their hands leave them in September. Even the most generous *fazendeiros* experience the same difficulty. According to the Director of Colonization, 40 per cent. to 60 per cent. of the colonists leave their *fazendas* annually. It is difficult to confirm this statement; but at least it is no exaggeration to say that a third of the families employed on the plantations leave their places from year to year. Towards September one meets them on the roads, most often travelling afoot; the man carrying a few household goods and the woman a newly born child, like the city labourers at the end of the season. One can imagine what a serious annoyance this instability of labour must be to the coffee-planter. Long before the harvest the planter is planning to fill up the gaps that will appear in the colony directly after the harvest. He secretly sends out hired recruiting agents to the neighbouring *fazendas* or to the nearest town; he employs for this purpose some of the shrewder colonists, to whom he pays a commission for every family engaged.

Finally, at the end of his resources, if he no longer has any hope of finding workmen in the neighbourhood who are experienced in plantation work, he decides to apply to the colonization agent in San Paolo, and resigns himself to the employment of an untrained staff, whom he will have to spend several months in training.

"The instability of agricultural labour is the most striking characteristic of rural life in the State of San Paolo. It is a result of the unusual and even artificial nature of the hasty development of coffee-planting."[29]

The colonists on the coffee-plantations are, in the main, Italians, of whom there may be perhaps three-quarters of a million in San Paolo.

The settlers or immigrants in Brazil, however, are not all of the San Paolo type, and in other parts of the Republic the condition of their life differs altogether from those of the coffee-plantation labourers. In Paraná, Rio Grande and elsewhere, very diverse pictures of colonial life may be painted, more independent in their colours, with less of the "rural proletariat." There are rural democracies of small holders in some instances, and a wide variety of products are cultivated, or small industries pursued.

In Paraná, the famous and valuable *maté* is largely grown, and the leaf of this small shrub—not unlike the ilex, or evergreen oak, is exported far and wide to Argentina, and other lands of the Plate, and to Chile, across the Cordillera. For Paraná, the *maté* is what coffee is for San Paolo.

COFFEE HARVEST, BRAZIL.

Vol. II. To face p. 150.

"*Maté* is not cultivated. It grows freely in the forest, and in the forest its leaves are harvested. As soon as plucked the leaves undergo a first preparation, which is designed principally to diminish their weight before transport, but also to prevent their fermenting or turning sour. They are dried at the fire, and are then packed in sacks which are sent to Curitiba, where improved mills reduce the leaves to powder, separate the various qualities, and deliver the product ready for consumption. Some colonists, more fortunate than others, found on their allotments large numbers of *maté*-trees; this meant for them a small fortune acquired without labour. The *maté*-leaf, or *the leaf*, as they call it in Paraná—a light but precious merchandise—bears the cost of transport more easily than maize; so that the owners of lots upon which *maté* is found are able to make a profit by the sale of their leaves. Such good fortune is unhappily rare.

"The great *hervaïs*, as they call the forest cantons where *maté* grows abundantly, are nearly all in the interior of the State; beyond the colonies, on that portion of the plateau which approaches the Paraná River; a country little known to geographers, but which, thanks to *maté*, is not lacking in importance nor economic vitality. At the season for plucking 'the leaf' it is intensely animated; a veritable army goes into camp, and all the forest paths are busy. From the eastern border the pack-mules carry their loads of leaves as far as the roads which lead to Curitiba, capital of the trade; and to the west the paths are no less busy. There are Paraguayans, coming to take part in the harvest, and Paraguayan smugglers, who seek to cross the river without being sighted by the Customs officials; for a large portion of the harvest is destined for the border regions of Paraguay and Misionès.

"In the *hervaïs*—whether public or private lands—the harvest is farmed out to contractors, who undertake to organize it. They employ a numerous staff. Each contractor constructs a hearth for drying the leaves, and this hearth becomes the centre of the little ephemeral world which lives for a few months in the heart of the forest, leading an isolated and laborious existence. Four or five tons of leaves are often prepared in a day. Some of the workers prune the trees; the others dry the leaves. The gangs are recruited from all over the State, and from the first day of harvest the Polish colonies furnish a good number of recruits. The men alone leave the colony, the women remaining to take care of the allotments. Some of the Poles are simple workmen, while those with more initiative are themselves contractors. All bring from the forests the money representing their wages or their profits, and on this money the colonies have managed to live."[30]

Here is a picture of the negroes on the sugar-producing lands and elsewhere.

"A small proportion of the land belongs to negroes. Small ownership among the negroes dates from before the abolition of slavery. The masters who freed slaves often gave them, with their liberty, a piece of land to ensure their subsistence. The negroes who have inherited these small holdings are to-day the best element of the black agricultural population. They form the majority of a class of peasant proprietors, tilling their land with their own hands, which also comprises mulattoes and even a few whites. This class is unfortunately too restricted.

"Taking them all in all, the negroes in the sugar-producing regions like Minas form a type of labourer of very indifferent economic value. The very sun assures them of many alimentary products, obtained without agricultural labour. Fish swarm in the marshes of the coast. A child will catch in one day enough to feed ten men. The fish, indeed, save the blacks from the obligation of regular labour. Although by no means the whole of the soil is under cultivation, certain sugar-producing districts are thus able to support a population of extraordinary density, swarming like ants in an ant-hill.

"In Bahia the sugar plantations have entirely disappeared. In Pernambuco the majority of the negroes live, as formerly, on the plantations. A large number, however, have crowded into the towns; for the negroes, who, in order to show their independence, have scattered far from the *fazendas* on which they used to live, none the less hate solitude, and are very eager for an urban life. In Pernambuco and Bahia the urban population is too large for the business capacity of the cities and the activity of the harbours. Around the cities properly so called stretch immense suburbs, vast villages where the negroes live, without very appreciable resources, among the mango and bread-fruit trees. It is amazing, on crossing a *fazenda* in Minas, or a Campos plantation, to see the number of negroes who can lodge and feed themselves on a minimum quantity of work. One feels the same astonishment in the large villages of the north. If you desire a boat, twenty boatmen dispute your custom. In Pernambuco market I remember having seen twenty merchants who had between them a stock of fruit which could have been carried in two baskets.

"To sum up: the moral and economic inferiority of the negro population of Brazil is incontestable. The puerility of the negroes is extreme. They have no foresight, and are innocent of any form of ambition, the sole motive-power of progress. They are modest in their desires and easily satisfied. Whoever has heard, in the streets of Bahia, the sincere, sonorous, joyful laughter of some negro woman cannot fail to have experienced the mixture of contempt, indulgence and envy with which this nation of children inspires the Caucasian. Their imagination is strong and nimble; their sentimental life active; intellectual life they have none. They are superstitious, and their devotion has supported and still supports the four hundred churches of Bahia.

"They amuse themselves with ardour. More than half their life is devoted to amusements and festivals. The circus is their favourite amusement. The wit of the clown keeps them happy for hours. Some of their festivals are connected with their agricultural labours. They were formerly celebrated on the *fazenda* by the slaves; they have survived slavery. In Minas the black workers still come, when the coffee harvest is over, bearing in their hands boughs of the coffee-tree, which they ornament with multi-coloured ribbons of paper, shouting for the master to give the signal for the rejoicings to commence."[31]

In Southern Brazil we may still see the picturesque figure in an old industry—the *gaucho* of the cattle-plains. The *gaucho*, or "cowboy," is a product of his calling, a creature of his kind. From childhood he has lived on horseback; has early learned all feats of wild horsemanship, including the throwing of the *riata*, or lasso, and the *boliadeira*, the latter a thong with a ball at each end which, dexterously thrown, winds around the legs of a fleeing animal and brings it to the ground. This form of lasso is peculiar to the South American *gaucho*, and is unknown to the *vaquero* of Mexico, whose marvellous exploits with the ordinary noosed lasso, or riata, we may have witnessed. Again, the *gaucho* will stem a charging bull by striking it across the muzzle with a short whip, and he seems quite fearless at the animal's onslaught upon him.

The life of this strange cattle-minder may be lived on the lonesome *pampa* for long periods. For his meat he may bring down a steer, cut off a portion of flesh with hide attached, and lay it in the embers of the camp fire, in rude cookery. He eats *farinha* with it, washed down with water, if his wine or *aguardiente* has given out, but follows it with the inevitable *maté*, the "Paraguayan tea." He will not live in the town, he is a creature of the plains. His wide-brimmed hat and silken or woollen poncho and huge coloured neck-handkerchief, raw hide boots, and enormous silver spurs, and other decorated trappings, are the habiliments he fancies best, and no ornate palace in Rio would tempt him to abandon his free and independent life.

Turning now to a different field; if the interests of the traveller in Brazil lie in the rich world of minerals, he will not find here so varied and historical a field as that we have traversed in the regions of the Cordillera. Yet Nature has not necessarily been niggardly even here. In centuries past much gold has been produced, in *placer* and other workings, and diamonds have been exported for nearly two centuries. One of the most famous gold mines of South America, indeed, the largest and most constant producer of any on this continent, is situated in the Republic, that of the St. John del Rey, whose workings are a matter of annual congratulation to its London shareholders, with its plentiful dividends, distributed with almost monotonous regularity to an amount approaching at times to half a million sterling per annum. The mine is of enormous depth.

Baser metals have also their possibilities here. Brazil has been endowed by the geological operation of Nature with immense deposits of iron, such as we certainly do not encounter in any other part of Latin America, and these we may survey in the department of Minas Geraes. Very high-grade ores of iron exist here—thousands of millions of tons. Unfortunately the country has little coal for purposes of smelting the ore, and the iron industry may be largely confined to that of export of the raw mineral.

Along the sandy coasts of Brazil another mineral, found of recent years to be of value, has been disposed. This is the peculiar monazite. There are, in addition, many other metals and minerals of commerce in various parts of the country: also petroleum. Perhaps the mining laws of Brazil have not been so favourable to the foreigner as those of the Spanish American Republics.

The general economic policy of Brazil, one which with greater or less intensity seems to be set before the Government and the intelligent classes, is a scheme of self-supplying trade, commerce and production in general, to produce its own food supplies, to manufacture its own goods, to be less dependent in these matters on the outside world. The magnificent and varied resources of the country are such as, as far as material is concerned, would render this policy possible of fulfilment as time goes on. It has been said by some observers that the Brazilian hates trade. Be it as it may, the country is very highly protected in a fiscal sense. It is a wealthy land, and undoubtedly has before it a future of such life and importance as at present it is impossible to picture in detail, but which might well be one of prosperity.

In Brazil there are innumerable matters of great interest, whether in town or country, whether in "the desert or the sown," which we have not space here to consider; and the traveller and observer will find material of the most varied and surprising nature to absorb his energies, be they in what field they may.

To the south, Brazil merges into those distinctive regions of the great plains and rivers of the Plate, which we now enter.

CHAPTER XIII
THE RIVER PLATE AND THE PAMPAS
ARGENTINA, URUGUAY AND PARAGUAY

The name of the River Plate, or the Rio de la Plata, is one which falls familiarly on English ears, or at least upon the hearing of those whose interests in finance, stock and share, and bank and railway of the South American shore, finds material of activity in the South American "market" in the city of London. They may not know the origin of its name, nor whence it comes or whither it flows. It is the "Silver River," named from the *plata*, or silver, which from the Inca Empire adventurers brought that way, and to-day it carries a stream of treasure to the pocket of the modern shareholder.

As to the Pampas—a word we also owe to the Inca tongue, this name must carry memories to many a Briton and inspiration to many another.

Here, then, we are bound for the Plate, towards whose mighty estuary a fleet of England's steamships constantly directs its course, together with craft from other European lands, bearing traveller, emigrants or merchandise; returning thence with the foods of half a hemisphere.

This mighty stream of the Plate, with its tributaries, is second only in size to the great Amazon in this continent. But how different is its destiny from that of the dark river of the Equator! If it rises amid the savage wildernesses, at least it flows through fruitful plains and waters the abodes of a great civilization.

Let us pay the small homage to the River Plate of first laying out the map upon our table, and so mark its winding curves and mazy courses. They come from mountain, from forest, from savage jungle; they sweep from north and west, pour over the cascades of Brazil, from the slopes of the far-off Andes, from the dim forests of Paraguay; they filter through the swamps of the Pilcomayo, a perilous and savage stream, all in the heart of a continent; the Paraná, the "Mother of the Sea," as the old Guarani Indians termed it, the Uruguay, the Paraguay, giving their names to those lands these full-flowing rivers caressingly encircle, all sweeping down to east and south, perilous or gentle, by foaming rapid or gentle current, past fertile fields and many a handsome town, pouring onwards for many a thousand mile, to empty into that remarkable vent of the South American waters and activity, the Plata Estuary.

A little over four hundred years ago, in 1516, the Spanish navigator, Juan de Solis, the chief pilot of Spain, bent upon that insistent search for a strait—

that elusive strait which in the minds of the geographers of that time showed a way to the real Indies and the East, but which none found, for the reason that Nature had not afforded one there—found the great estuary of what is now La Plata, a hundred and fifty miles wide. Back to Spain with the news he went, returning with a further mandate to explore, when he sailed up the great waters for three hundred miles.

Here he thought to capture some of the Indians of the "Mother of Waters," and to take them with him to Spain. But they, resenting the pretension, ambushed the explorer's party, and de Solis was killed. Four years later Magellan essayed the passage.

But the name of La Plata did not result from these voyages. It was Sebastian Cabot, the Englishman in the service of Spain, who, later, ascending the great estuary then known as the Mar Dulce, or fresh-water sea, discovered the Paraná, and, following it and the Paraguay River upstream, and landing where the city of Asuncion now stands, found the Guaranis wearing silver ornaments, and from these baubles—which, however, came in reality not from the district itself but from across the Andes, from the still unknown Inca Empire of Peru—gave the name of the Plate or Plata River.

Its wealth to-day comes not from precious metals, but from the bounties of Nature in the vegetable and animal world: the wealth of corn and cattle.

BUENOS AYRES.

Vol. II. To face p. 160.

Cabot established a settlement at San Espiritu. The rumours of a great, rich, unknown empire fired his imagination. Then he returned to Spain for means to open up communication with the lands beyond the Andes. But in his absence the garrison was massacred by the Indians. A chief of the Timbus became enamoured of a certain Spanish lady among the few colonists, and he, striving to gain possession of her, caused the treacherous murder of the garrison. Two years after Cabot's return to Europe, the astounding news of Pizarro's conquest of Peru arrived, in 1532, and adventurous spirits were fired with the desire themselves to set forth on similar quests of gold and fortune. Among these spirits of the times was the Marquis of Mendoza, and the story of how he failed in reaching Peru forms one of the interesting pages of history in this picturesque period. Mendoza, on February 2, 1534, founded Buenos Ayres, which has grown to the vast and wealthy Argentine capital[32] of to-day. Some of Mendoza's people, who had survived the dangers to which many fell victims, founded Asuncion, the first Spanish American interior capital, to-day the capital of the Republic of Paraguay.

But let us turn to our map.

The Paraná River, rising in Goyaz, in Southern Brazil, flows for 1,600 miles to its confluence with the Paraguay, and thence 600 miles to the Plate. Its main branch, the Paranahyba, drains a region but little known on the southern watershed of Brazil; and there are many other tributaries which, although obstructed in places by rapids, may be navigated in canoes, carrying the venturesome traveller into regions wild and remote, amid the rocky valleys and dense forests beyond the Tropic of Capricorn. There are magnificent cascades on these rivers, and dreadful rapids and profound gorges, cut out by the river in the rocks, through which the torrent plunges with frightful velocity, its roar awakening the echoes of the woods and the broken wilderness.

By the main stream of the Paraná our steamer, of not more than twelve feet draught, reaches the city of Paraná, and here we are 300 miles above Buenos Ayres. Rosario, which we shall have passed on the voyage upstream, is 185 miles from Buenos Ayres, and may be reached by larger vessels of fifteen feet draught.

To proceed now onwards upstream to Asuncion, our steamer must not draw more than ten feet of water, or it will strand on the shallows, but here we are little short of a thousand miles from the Plate, in the very heart of the continent. To reach Asuncion, after five days' steaming up this full-flowing river, we have entered a region of gorgeous forests and beautiful backwaters, the home of the *Victoria regia* lily and of bright plumaged kingfishers and of the alligator. Away to the west lies the great Chaco plain or desert, and the Pilcomayo River. The elevation of the town is about 250 feet above sea-level, and thus we have ascended to that altitude on the current.

To ascend the Pilcomayo River, the western affluent of the Plata, will demand more effort than the easy passage of Paraná. It is a stream tortuous and of great length, but of little volume in comparison with those great streams which irrigate the lands we have described.

Unexplored in part, this wild waterway has a sinister reputation by reason of the disasters which have befallen the early attempts to navigate its waters. Its headwaters are in the Andes of Bolivia, in the region of Sucre and Potosi, and from thence to the edge of the Chaco the river falls 8,000 feet in 350 miles. It filters through a vast and dismal swamp a hundred miles across, and traverses numerous lagoons. Racing down the mountain slopes the Pilcomayo crosses the great plain of the Chaco and pours into the Paraguay River not far from the town of Asuncion. Many tributaries, many bifurcations, divide and lessen its current on its winding course, which at times wanders about in search of new channels, eroding and washing away the soil of the Pampas; a desolate and capricious stream. But one valuable asset of this and kindred waterways in the future, we may reflect, will be in the hydraulic power it is capable of furnishing, an asset indeed of value, to be developed some day, in a region where Nature has omitted to furnish motive power in the more accessible form of coalfields. Moreover, as this part of the continent becomes more settled under the growing exigencies of civilization, there is the valuable function of irrigation to be developed.

A waterway of a very different character is the Uruguay River. We may trace its course for a thousand miles, from where its many headstreams flow down the slope of the Brazilian Serra do Mar, or maritime range, leaving which the river runs through beautiful country, open and hilly, for a long distance. Great cataracts interrupt the course, and, in places, contracted in width between deep, thickly wooded banks, the stream is of great depth, and its waters, flowing over a sandstone bottom, are generally clear, with little silt. It is subject to heavy floods by reason of the rains in its upper basin, which at times submerge the rocks which obstruct its current. But, apart from its upper reaches, broad and full-flowing, the Uruguay encircles the Republic whose name it bears on its western side, and, falling into the Plate, affords, in conjunction with the sea, a water-frontage on three sides of the State, and is navigable for 200 miles from its mouth as far as the towns of Salta and Paysandu. Many hundreds of miles of the river are navigable in smaller craft, affording valuable waterways for the inhabitants on its banks.

The enormous quantity of water of this great fluvial system, pouring into the Plate, give that estuary a greater volume than the great Mississippi. At its mouth the Plate is 138 miles wide, and opposite Montevideo, the Uruguayan capital, its bosom is still 57 miles broad, whilst, narrowing, it is 25 miles across at the confluence of the Paraná and Uruguay.

The port of Buenos Ayres, however, is not favoured by Nature as regards the depth of its harbour, which is only kept open for ocean steamers by constant dredging. This commercial and maritime navel of South America thus suffers from a considerable disadvantage. An outlay amounting to over £12,000,000 has been necessary to render the docks of the great entrepôt always accessible to the numerous ocean steamers which make it their haven. Before the artificial channels were dredged, such vessels as drew over fifteen feet of water could not approach within twelve miles of the port, and unloading was laboriously performed from launches.

It cannot be said that the shores of the estuary of the Plate River, as we approach Buenos Ayres, impress themselves upon the mind by reason of their beauty. The city stands on a flat plain, without background of hills or other pleasing topographical feature, and its surroundings are, in consequence, low and monotonous. The main objects to break the skyline are the unhandsome forms of giant grain elevators—those structures more familiar to the traveller from the United States, where they abound. Other outstanding objects are the huge slaughter-houses, like those of Chicago. The aspect of the place is, in fact, strictly utilitarian. When, moreover, we read the enthusiastic descriptions of the city, of its wealth, its public buildings, its boulevards, we must recollect that these features lie beyond the poor, clustered dwellings near the water-front, of folk who, largely necessitous immigrants, have been unable or unwilling to proceed into the interior, whether by reason of disillusion or from the abuses they fear will be practised upon them. The Argentine Government has done much towards the settlement of the Republic, but the economic conditions and humane direction of immigrants is one which no Government has yet been able sufficiently to compass. These considerations, however, may be left for further remark elsewhere in these pages. Buenos Ayres is a handsome city, a source of pride to Argentina, and an instance of the civic possibilities of the Spanish American race.

Before reaching Buenos Ayres we shall have entered Montevideo, the capital of Uruguay, the smallest of the South American States, a seaport and city more beautifully situated, extending around the shore of its bay, with a rocky headland jutting out in the west. Here the Atlantic breezes blow freely over the city—situated on its rolling lands, a city one of the cleanest in the world and one of the most pleasing in South America.

MAR DEL PLATA.

The sky of Montevideo seems unfailingly blue, the sun shines constantly, the temperature is that of summer, rarely falling below 50° even in winter. The handsome harbour has been rendered safe for vessels, and docks were built under large expenditure: work carried out by national funds, without the need of a foreign loan—that inevitable Spanish American method of performing a public work. Rio de Janeiro and Buenos Ayres have their advantages, æsthetic or commercial, but Montevideo, in point of climate and other amenities, is their leader.

On the opposite shore of the estuary stands the Argentine city of La Plata, capital of Argentina, a few miles inland from the port of Ensenada, a provincial capital founded in 1882. The model taken in its town-planning was Washington, but the streets are of a width so considerable as to give an air of disproportion, in conjunction with the low brick buildings. Here we may visit the most important museum in South America, ethnographical and archæological.

But to return to Uruguay.

We shall not confuse in our minds the two Republics of Uruguay and Paraguay, as is often done. The one is progressive and wealthy, the other backward and poor. Their boundaries are far from each other, separated by portions of Brazil and Argentina, but they are united by the great waterways of the Plate, as we have already seen.

If Uruguay is a small country in point of area, being about the size of the British Isles, which is not large in comparison with the vast areas of territory of her neighbours on the Continent, the Republic contains much that is important, both as regards its own life and development and its relations with foreign lands. As an indication of the latter element, we may recollect the many millions sterling of English money invested here in public works and other matters.

The history of the land has been a chequered one. War and peace have alternately succeeded each other ever since independence was gained, and the soil has had its full baptism of the blood of its own sons. But much of this customary dreadful history of Spanish America has here been tinged by the patriotic spirit of the Uruguayans, their strong national mind and their individualism.

The strange mixture of idealism and cruelty which is found in the outstanding figures of Spanish American revolutionary history is, we may here reflect, remarkable. We find men who have lived the dreadful lives of guerilla chiefs, with their hands not merely stained with blood, but their honour besmirched with the most horrible deeds—deeds of torture, of treason, of massacre, of rape, of robbery—sometimes enunciating the most philosophical and beautiful sentiments or enduring aphorisms. The dividing line between bloodshed and cruelty and philosophy is, in Spanish America, a very narrow one, and the Spanish American may be called upon to cross it perhaps between breakfast and lunch. We find such figures and situations in every one of the twenty States of Iberian America, from Mexico to Uruguay.

A national hero of Uruguay was Artigas, an ex-smuggler who rose to be Dictator over a vast territory; who rose with dramatic rapidity in the turbulent times of the War of Independence and the civil struggles that followed. It is not here suggested that Artigas was of the character described in the former paragraph, although some historians have painted him in the darkest colours, but opportunity is taken to show the varied sides of such characters, in their enunciations of lofty sentiments. When, in 1815, Artigas was endowed by the Montevideo Government with the title of "Captain-General, Protector and Patron of the Liberty of the Nation," he replied: "Titles are the phantoms of States. Let us teach our countrymen to be virtuous. It is thus I have retained the title of a simple citizen." Now comes the flash of philosophy. "The day will come," said this guerilla chief, "when men will act from a sense of duty, and when they will devote their best interests to the honour of their fellow men."

Here is a further page from the early history of Independence on the River Plate:

> "Artigas was now encamped for the first time with a translated nation and an independent army of his own. The condition of both was grimly tragic, pathetically humorous. For fourteen months almost the only shelter,

that served for all alike, was afforded by the branches of the trees and the boards of the carts that had brought them. As for the army, it was composed of strangely heterogeneous elements. Honest countryfolk rubbed shoulders with professional criminals and cut-throats; Indians from the destroyed Jesuit missions went side by side with fierce-faced Gauchos; while townsmen, negroes and a few adventurous foreigners made up the mixed gathering.

"The men were in deadly earnest, since the example of Artigas seems to have inspired even the most depraved with a spark from his own fire. Had it been otherwise they would undoubtedly have succumbed to the disadvantages with which they had to contend. Arms were scarce. A certain favoured few were possessed of muskets and swords; but the weapon in chief use was the lance, the national arm of River Plate folk, the point of which, here at Ayui, was usually fashioned from the blade of shears or a knife, or from the iron of some other agricultural instrument. Many, however, had perforce to be content with a long knife, with the lasso and the sling—the *boleadores*—as subsidiary weapons. Yet even these proved by no means despicable in the hands of the men whose sole garment was the ragged remnant of a poncho tied about the waist, and who exercised with poles in preparation for the time when a musket should be in their hands.

"It was with the aid of an army such as this that Artigas would cross the river to make his incursions among the hills of his native country, and would engage Portuguese and Spaniards alike in battles from which the desperate and motley companies of men would frequently emerge victorious. Artigas was now assisted by numerous minor chiefs, many of whom were of a character quite unfitted to stand the light of day. Otorgues and Andresito were the most noted of these. The methods of the former were utterly brutal. Although the fact is discredited, he is credited by many with the order to a subaltern officer to 'cut the throats of two Spaniards a week in order to preserve the morale. Failing Spaniards, take two Buenos Ayrens for the purpose'!

"Andresito was an Indian from the deserted Jesuit missions who commanded a considerable force of his own race. He appears to have interspersed his dark deeds with some evidence of better qualities and even of a grim humour. A coarse instance of this latter is supplied when he entered the town of Corrientes in the heyday of Artigas's power. On this occasion the Indian troops behaved with no little restraint towards the terrified inhabitants, and contented themselves with levying contributions towards the clothing of the almost naked army. This accomplished, Andresito determined to exhibit the social side of his temperament. He organized several religious dramas, and followed these by a ball in honour of the principal residents of the town. These, however, failed to attend, their reluctance to dancing with Indians overcoming their prudence. On learning the reason from some crassly honest person, the enraged Andresito caused these too particular folk to be mustered in the main plaza of the town. There he obliged the men to scour the roadway, while the ladies were made to dance with the Indian troops.

"Although no merit or subtlety can be claimed for such methods, they at all events stand apart from the rest in their lack of bloodthirstiness. Compared with the sentiments revealed in a proclamation of Otorgues in taking possession of Montevideo, the procedure at Corrientes seems innocuous and tame. One of the clauses of this document decrees the execution within two hours of any citizen who should speak or write in favour of any other government, while the same fate was promised to one 'who should directly or indirectly attack the liberty of the province'! The humour in the employment of the word 'liberty' is, of course, totally unconscious.

"Such proclamations, naturally, served purely and simply as a licence for convenient murder. Employing lieutenants of the kind, it is little wonder that much of the guilt of their accumulated deeds should be undeservedly heaped upon Artigas's head. Not that the Commander-in-Chief himself was inclined to put a sentimental value upon human life; indeed, a delicacy on this point would be impossible in one who had passed through the scenes of his particular calling. In any case his hatred of robbery was deep-rooted and sincere. After the execution of three criminals of this type, he proclaims to his people at Ayui: 'My natural aversion to all crime, especially to the horrible one of robbery, and my desire that the army should be composed of honourable citizens ... has moved me to satisfy justice by means of a punishment as sad as it is effectual.' A little later he makes a similar appeal, adding, 'if there be remaining amongst you one who does not harbour sentiments of honour, patriotism and humanity, let him flee far from the army he dishonours'! Here we get the flowers of the south, earnestly thrown, but alighting in too earthy a bed! The poor army, with its impoverished, ragged loin-cloths, and with its lassos and slings, undoubtedly valued the occasional luxury of a full stomach at least as highly as the abstract virtues. Yet they probably heard the words with sincere admiration, feeling an added pride in their beloved leader who could employ such phrases. In any case—whether as a result of punishments or proclamations—the crime of robbery soon became rare almost to extinction within the sphere of Artigas's influence.

"The war itself was each month growing more savage in character. Such virtues as the Uruguayan army possessed were recognized least of all by the Spaniards. Elio, the Viceroy, had erected a special gallows in Montevideo for the benefit of any prisoners that might be captured, while Vigodet, his successor, endeavoured to strike terror by measures of pure barbarity. By his order a body of cavalry scoured the countryside, slaying all those suspected of Artiguenian leanings, and exposing the quartered portions of their bodies at prominent places by the roadside. Each patriot, moreover, carried a price upon his head. It is not to be wondered at that the Uruguayan forces made reprisals, and that corpses replaced prisoners of war."[33]

These matters took place a century or more ago, as did the picturesque incidents of the *Treinta y Tres*, the thirty-three resolutes who swore to liberate their country, when the news of the Battle of Ayacucho, in Peru, on the distant Andes, had reached the land of the Plate and the Pampas.

"The rejoicings that the victory of Ayacucho aroused in the capital of Argentina stirred to the depth both Lavalleja and a company of fellow-exiles from the Banda Oriental. A meeting of these patriots was held on the spot, the result of which was an enthusiastic determination to place their own country upon the same footing as the rest. Doubtless many hundreds of similar gatherings had already been effected—and concluded by vapourings of thin air. But the spirit of these men who had thus come together was of another kind. Having sworn solemnly to free their country, action followed hot-foot on the heels of words. A couple of their number were sent at once to Uruguay to prepare the minds of a trusted few, while the rest made preparations for the expedition that was to follow.

"The mission of the two deputies proved successful. They returned to Buenos Ayres, the bearers of many promises of support and co-operation. Nothing now remained but to take the first irrevocable step in the campaign that was to bloom out from this very humble seed.

"'Treinta y Tres' has now developed into a proper name in the Banda Oriental; for the number of men who started out from Buenos Ayres for the sake of Uruguay was thirty-three. The name has now been locally immortalized. Among the infinite variety of objects that it endows may be counted a province, a town, innumerable plazas and streets and a brand of cigarettes.

"There is certainly nothing that is intrinsically humorous in the adventures of these noble men who set out for their patriotic purpose in the face of such terrible risks. Yet as a specimen of the constitution of the armies of the South American factions at this period a survey of the grades held by the small gathering is illuminating. In the first place the diminutive expedition had for its Commander-in-Chief Colonel Juan Antonio Lavalleja, who had beneath him three majors and four captains. These in turn were supported by three lieutenants, an ensign, a sergeant, a corporal and a guide. The remaining eighteen constituted the rank and file of the force—in fact, the Army proper.

"The little expedition so overwhelmingly officered set out from Buenos Ayres, proceeding northward along the Argentine shore. Reaching a point where the river had become comparatively narrow, they embarked in small boats, and launched out on the Uruguay at dead of night. A gale obliged them to seek refuge on a friendly island,

and caused a day's delay. But the next evening they embarked once more, and reached in safety the beach of La Agraciada on their native shore. There they unfurled their chosen tricoloured banner, and swore once again to attain liberty or death.

"The expedition was now actually on the scene of its mission, and shortly after daybreak it began its march to the north. During the course of a few hours they collected *en route* reinforcements of forty able-bodied and armed Orientales.

"Proceeding steadily onwards, the gallant little army, officers and all, found itself in the neighbourhood of the small town of Dolores, better known formerly as San Salvador. This was held by a garrison of eighty men in the service of Brazil. Determined to inflict a first decisive blow, Lavalleja led his men onwards to the attack. The moment chanced to be especially propitious, since the officers and principal men in the town had attended a dance on the previous night. So great had been the delights of the *baile* that the principal men had found it necessary to continue their repose long into the morning—a circumstance that is not unknown even to this day.

"Had it not been for an error on the part of the patriot guide the town would undoubtedly have been captured by surprise and taken almost without a blow. As it was, the official chanced to mistake the situation of a ford in an intervening small river. This necessitated a lengthy march along the banks ere a place suitable for the passage was found, and the presence of the small company with the tricoloured flag was discovered with amazement by the inhabitants.

"Thus ere Lavalleja's expedition had succeeded in crossing the stream there had been moments of wild bustle in Dolores. Officers sprang out of bed to gird on their swords in haste; soldiers ran to assemble with uniforms even more than usually awry, while the municipal officers doubtless ran to and fro in aimless confusion. Nevertheless by the time that the turmoil was at an end the garrison had had an opportunity to muster, and to sally out against the advancing band that had not yet gained the town."[34]

To-day considerable prosperity is seen among those who hold power and place, and control lands and commerce in this enterprising Republic; and the people of Uruguay have evolved their own personality.

> "The hospitality of the higher classes is proverbial. Indeed, reputable conviviality of all kinds is at a premium. In Montevideo the occasions for the giving of banquets are numberless. Thus if a man has achieved something in particular it is necessary that a banquet should mark the event, if he has expressed his intention of achieving anything in particular, a banquet forms the appropriate prelude to the work, and if he has failed to do anything in particular, there is nothing like one of these selfsame banquets to console him for the disappointment.
>
> "It is, in fact, much to the Uruguayan's credit that he contrives to extract a vast deal of enjoyment from life in a comparatively homely and unostentatious manner. The race meetings here, for instance, are most pleasant functions, although the horses are not burdened with the responsibility of those tremendous stakes that prevail in some other parts. The theatres, too, although they obtain the services of excellent companies, are moderate in their charges—moderate considering the usual scale that prevails in South America, that is to say.
>
> "The advent of a prosperity, however, that now seems more definite than ever before has produced a similar effect upon household expenditure as in the neighbouring countries. The cost of living has risen by leaps and bounds during the past two or three years—a fact that salaried foreigners resident in the country have found out to their somewhat acute inconvenience. In the Campo, naturally enough, this phenomenon of ways and means has not occurred. When live stock and acres are numbered only by the thousand such annoying matters as house-rent and the butcher's bill fail to carry any significance. Nevertheless, in Montevideo the former has practically doubled itself within the last half-dozen years, and all similar items have followed suit as a matter of course. But the rise in the price of land signifies prosperity, and is at all events welcome enough to those directly interested in the soil.

MONTEVIDEO: THE PLAZA AND THE HARBOUR.

Vol. II. To face p. 178.

"South America, taken as a whole, is a continent whose inhabitants are not a little addicted to ostentation. The phase is natural enough in view of the conditions that obtain in so many of the Republics. In the case of the pastoral countries, even in quite modern times the broad lands had lain comparatively valueless until the introduction of the freezing process for meat and the opening up of the great wheat and maize areas sent up the price of the soil by leaps and bounds. Yet even prior to this era a certain amount of prosperity had prevailed, and young South Americans had become accustomed up to a certain point to wend their way for educational purposes to France and to England, and thus to assimilate European ideas with those that prevailed at the time in the Republics of the south.

"The sudden advent of overflowing wealth thus found them to a great extent prepared to introduce the most high-flown of modern ideas into the life of their own country. No doubt the very consciousness of these riches that, head for head, undoubtedly far surpass that of the dwellers in the Old Continent, caused the South

Americans to fling aside the last vestige of pastoral simplicity and to make the roots of this great wealth of theirs bud out into residential palaces and entertainments of a rather fabulous order. Since they had shown clearly enough that their material gains had surpassed those of Europe, what more natural than that they should endeavour to prove with equal conclusiveness their ability to outshine the continent of their ancestors in the ornamentation and luxuries that follow automatically in the footsteps of fortune! Surely the trait is nothing beyond the proof of the healthy rivalry.

"The Oriental is undoubtedly a man of deeds; but in his case the tendency to action is not effected at the expense of speech. He is, indeed, a born orator, and on the slightest provocation will burst forth into a stream of eloquence that can be quite indefinitely continued. In any case, it is pleasant enough to listen to the resounding periods in which the customary lofty sentiments are couched, but it is as well to bear in mind that the oratorical effort may mean very much—or very little.

"Uruguay, more especially its capital, is well-found in the matter of femininity. Indeed, ever since it became a full-blown city Montevideo has been celebrated for its pretty women. This fortunate state of affairs has now become a well-recognized fact, in which the masculine portion of the community takes an even greater pride than does the sex more directly involved. Should a patriotic Montevidean be engaged in conversation with an interested foreigner, the chances are that it will not be long ere the confident question is asked: 'And our señoritas, what is your opinion of them?'

"In such a case there can be only one opinion—or expression of opinion. Conscience may be salved by the reflection that it is as difficult to find a woman without some stray claim to beauty as it is to light upon a dame of sixty without a grey hair. In both cases the feature may be hard to see. If so, it must be taken for granted. In the case of the Montevidean señorita no such feat of the imagination is necessary. To the far-famed graces of her sisters throughout South America she adds the freshness of complexion and the liveliness of temperament that are characteristic of the land.

"Indeed, to conceive these lighter virtues, added to the natural Spanish stateliness, is to picture a very bewitching feminine consummation. Much has been written concerning the señoritas of Uruguay, and yet not a line too much. Their own kith and kin have sung their praises with all the tremendous hyperbole of which the Spanish tongue is capable. White hands, bright eyes, raven hair, and a corresponding remainder of features that resemble all pleasant things from a dove to the moon—the collection of local prose and verse on the subject is justifiably enormous.

"The Montevidean lady has now, of course, become essentially modern. She rides in a motor-car, plays the piano instead of the guitar, and has exchanged the old order in general for the new. Yet the same vivacity, courage and good looks remain—which is an excellent and beneficial thing for Montevideo and its inhabitants. Indeed, the beach of Poçitos or the sands of Ramirez shorn of their female adornment would be too terrible a disaster to contemplate even on the part of the most hardened Oriental. And at this point it is advisable to forsake for the present the more intimate affairs of the people, leaving the last word to the ladies, as, indeed, is only fitting—and frequently inevitable.

"The Uruguayan's appreciation of pleasant Nature is made abundantly clear in the surroundings of the capital. The city, as a matter of fact, is set about with quite an exceptional number of pleasant resorts both inland and upon the shore. Of the former the Prado park and the pleasure suburb of Colón are the best known. The Prado is reached within half an hour from the centre of the city by means of tramway-car. Situated on the outskirts of the town, the park is very large and genuinely beautiful. Groves of trees shading grassy slopes, beds of flowers glowing by the sides of ponds and small lakes, walks, drives and sheltered seats—the place possesses all these commendable attributes, and many beyond.

"The Montevidean is very proud of the Prado, and he has sufficient reason for his pride. He has taken a portion of the rolling country, and has made of the mounds and hills the fairest garden imaginable. The place would be remarkable if for nothing more than the great variety and number of its trees, both Northern and sub-tropical. But here this fine collection forms merely the background for the less lofty palms, bamboos and all the host of the quainter growths, to say nothing of the flowering shrubs and the land and water blossoms. One may roam for miles in and out of the Prado vegetation, only to find that it continues to present fresh aspects and beauties all the while.

"The expedition to Colón is a slightly more serious one, since, the spot being situated some eight miles from the centre of the town, the journey by tramcar occupies an hour or so. As much that is typical of the outskirts of Montevideo is revealed by the excursion, it may be as well to describe it with some detail.

"It is only when once fairly launched upon a journey of the kind that the true extent of Montevideo and the length of its plane-shaded avenues proper become evident. Nevertheless, as the car mounts and dips with the undulation of the land, the unbroken streets of houses come to an end at length, giving way to the first *quintas*—the villas set within their own grounds. The aspect of these alone would suffice to convince the passing stranger of the real wealth of the capital. Of all styles of architecture, from that of the bungalow to the more intricate structure of many pinnacles and eaves, many of them are extremely imposing in size and luxurious to a degree. A moral to the newcomer in Montevideo should certainly be: Own a quinta in the suburbs; or, if you cannot, get to know the owner of a quinta in the suburbs, and stay with him!

"But if you would see these surroundings of Montevideo at their very best, it is necessary to journey there in October—the October of the Southern Hemisphere, when the sap of the plants is rising to counterbalance its fall in the North. The quintas then are positive haunts of delight—nothing less. Their frontiers are frequently marked by blossoming may, honeysuckle and rose-hedges, while bougainvillæa, wistaria and countless other creepers blaze from the walls of the houses themselves.

"As for the gardens, they have overflowed into an ordered riot of flower. The most favoured nooks of Madeira, the *Midi* of France, and Portugal would find it hard to hold their own in the matter of blossoms with this far Southern land. Undoubtedly, one of the most fascinating features here is the mingling of the hardy and homely plants with the exotic. Thus great banks of sweet-scented stock will spread themselves beneath the broad-leaved palms, while the bamboo spears will prick up lightly by the ivy-covered trunk of a Northern tree—a tree whose parasite is to be marked and cherished, for ivy is, in general, as rare in South America as holly, to say nothing of plum-pudding, though it is abundant here. Spreading bushes of lilac mingle their scent with the magnolia, orange, myrtle and mimosa, until the crowded air seems almost to throb beneath the simultaneous weight of the odours. Then down upon the ground, again, are periwinkles, pansies and marigolds, rubbing petals with arum-lilies, carnations, hedges of pink geranium, clumps of tree-marguerites and wide borders of cineraria. From time to time the suggestions of the North are strangely compelling. Thus, when the heavy flower-cones of the horse-chestnut stand out boldly next to the snow-white circles of the elder-tree, with a grove of oaks as a background, it is with something akin to a shock that the succeeding clumps of paraiso and eucalyptus-trees, and the fleshly leaves of the aloe and prickly-pear bring the traveller back to reality and the land of warm sunshine.

"But it is time to make an end to this long list of mere growths and blossoms. The others must be left to the imagination, from the green fig-bulbs to the peach-blossom and guelder-roses. Let it suffice to say that a number of these gardens are many acres in extent, and that you may distribute all these flowers—and the far larger number that remain unchronicled—in any order that you will.

"As the open country appears in the wider gaps left between the remoter quintas, and the space between the halting-places of the tram is correspondingly lengthened, the speed of a car becomes accelerated to a marked degree. The cottages that now appear at intervals at the side of the road are trim and spotlessly white. They are, almost without exception, shaded by the native ombú-tree, and are surrounded with trellis work of vines and with fig-trees, while near by are fields of broad beans and the extensive vineyards of commerce."[35]

Montevideo, we remark, is a city whose population may soon approximate to the figure of half a million. It is fortunate, moreover, in possessing good roads around it, for the country—unlike Argentina—is seamed with good stone for highway building, and thus the surrounding landscape may readily be surveyed.

Before leaving Uruguay, we should cast a glance towards its *Campo*, the lands of its Pampas.

"The Uruguayan Campo is not to be described without a certain amount of hesitation. It would be simple enough for one who had caught only a distant passing glimpse of the land of the pastures to put down the country without further ado as rolling grass upland watered by many streams. That such is the foundation of the Campo is undeniable. Nevertheless to begin and end with such a phrase would be equivalent to a description of the peacock as a bird who wears coloured feathers.

"The subtle charms of the Uruguayan Campo are not to be discerned through the medium of the bioscope-like glimpses that so many travellers obtain of it. Very rightly, it refuses to reveal itself fully until a certain amount of familiarity has justified a nearer acquaintance. From an æsthetic point of view it certainly holds far more than might be expected from a country of such comparatively limited attributes.

"If you desire to watch the moods of this rural Banda Oriental, ride out to mount one of the highest shoulders of the downland, and wait there, either in the saddle or out of it. You will obtain little sympathy in the task. Eccentric to the mind of the estancieros, frankly mad in the eagle eyes of the Gaucho—a calm survey of the Campo is worth all such merely human depreciation!

"The aspect of the country in the immediate neighbourhood of where the observer has taken his stand will be green in the main, although the unbroken verdure by no means obtains throughout. Here and there the ground is strongly marked by the occasional heaps of stones that come jostling to the surface, and that recline in the fashion of small bleak islands in the midst of the green waves. But, should the time be spring, these latter are themselves flecked frequently almost to the extinction of their own colouring. The great purple bands and patches of the *flor morala* lie thickly upon the land. These, however, stand apart, since where they glow the serried ranks of blossom permit no others to raise their heads.

"But these, though the boldest of their kind, are by no means the sole occupants of the landscape. Indeed, one of the chief characteristics of the Banda Oriental Campo is the wealth of beautiful and comparatively lowly plants that grow amidst the grasses. They are of the type of English blossoms, peering out shyly from between the green blades, blowing purely and sweetly in their innocence of the heavy sickliness of the Tropics. It is where the ground is chiefly dotted with these fresh flowers that the smile of the Campo is most brilliant.

"So much for the immediate surroundings up to the point where the more intricate markings become merged in the broader tints of the landscape. Down in the hollows are bands of dark, close green formed by the trees that shade the streams. With scarcely a break in the narrow walls of verdure they run from valley to valley, accurately defining the banks of the small rivers whose waters they conceal. Within these leafy lanes lurk the only spots upon the Campo, save for the rare woodland, that do not stare frankly upwards, exposing all their earthly soul to the blue sky.

"Away in the far distance there is a magic glamour. There the lands are no longer green to the eye. The soft waves, as they rise and dip in an accumulation of folds towards the final horizon line, are bathed in warm purple. The Banda Oriental has been called 'the purple land' by one who knew it well, and never was a name better applied. Without the foreground—that is itself strongly purpled by the banks of the *flor morala*—all is purple and mystic. The land has its ordinary mirages as well; but here is one that at all times confronts the traveller—that wonderful land of the horizon that, unattainable, dies farther away as it is approached.

"Yet, notwithstanding its soft romance, the place is essentially alive. It is a blowy haunt of clean fresh airs that sweep the slopes and open valleys to billow the grass tops and to refresh mankind. It is amidst such surroundings that the Oriental of the country dwells. His type is not very numerous, it is true, and—although the dearth of houses suits the landscape itself most admirably—the scarcity of habitation is a little lamentable in so wealthy and pleasant a land. It is practically certain, as a matter of fact, that the pastures will bear more roots in the near future than they have ever known in the past; but in the meanwhile it is necessary to take them as they are, and their inhabitants as well.

"Of these inhabitants the true *paisano*, the Gaucho, decidedly claims the chief share of attention. The Gaucho of the Banda Oriental is not to be confused with his brethren of the neighbouring countries. In appearance he presents perhaps the finest specimen amongst the various kindred families of his race. He is taller in stature, and, if possible, even more athletic in his lithe frame than his neighbour. His complexion, moreover, though frequently dusky and invariably tanned, is peculiarly wholesome and fresh. It was inevitable that the blowy downlands should have produced a fitting and appropriate breed of amazingly healthy, hardy and fearless men to whom the art of horsemanship has become second nature, while the occasional enforced spells of pedestrianism have degenerated into a mere unwelcome accident of life.

"The temperament of the Uruguayan Gaucho shows corresponding distinction from that of the rest. It goes without saying that he is strongly imbued with the grim dignity of the race. Silent austerity here, however, is modified by lighter traits. In the same way as the higher social member of his country, he is more easily moved to laughter than his neighbours, and indulges from time to time in frank outbursts of joviality.

"For practical purposes it is necessary to regard this child of the Campo from three standpoints—from that of the worker, the player and the fighter. It is rare enough that one of them is not called upon to fill all these three rôles on a good many occasions during his lifetime. As stock-rider, he has proved his courage, fidelity and honesty of purpose to the full; his moments of recreation are taken up by equestrian sports, guitar-playing and chance affairs of the heart, whilst in warfare he has had only too many opportunities of displaying his reckless brilliancy—frequently, it must be admitted, at the cost of discipline and order.

"In his private quarrels the Argentine Gaucho will bottle up his wrath until his overflowing passion culminates without warning in the rapid knife thrust or revolver shot. The conclusion of a serious dispute between his Uruguayan brethren will almost certainly be the same; but the tragic climax will be approached in quite another fashion. The atmospheric effervescence of the Banda Oriental will enter into the case. There will be shouting, vociferation and not a little abuse. Not until a fair exchange of all this has been bandied to and fro will come the flash of steel or flame—and the red stain upon the grasses of the Campo.

"That these dwellers upon the downlands should prove themselves born fighters is no matter for surprise. For the dusky side of their ancestry they claim the Charrúa Indians, the fiercest and most warlike of all the tribes in the neighbouring provinces. With this strain added to the blood of the old Spaniards, and the mixture fostered and nourished by the breezy hills, the result has been a being whose keen sense of dignity and honour were ever in the very active custody of knife or lance." But let us change the scene.

"The first two hundred miles of the Uruguay represent a particularly noble highway of waters, far broader and more imposing, indeed, than the equivalent stretch of the Paraná. Ocean-going vessels here penetrate to Paysandú, and beyond it to the Lemco port of Colón on the Argentine shore, while the really magnificent steamers of the River King, Mihanovich, produce their finest specimens to ply to and fro here. But, as the banks of the stream contain not only some of the most fertile lands of the Republic, but much of interest beyond, it is worth while to follow its course, beginning at Montevideo itself, which, as a matter of fact, is somewhat to anticipate the waters of the true Uruguay.

"By the quayside of the capital are grouped three or four of the Mihanovich craft, large, two-funnelled vessels with an imposing array of decks surmounted by an unusually spacious promenade that crowns the whole. One of these is bound for Salto—or rather for the Argentine town of Concordia that lies opposite that port—but just now it is not advisable to be tied hard and fast to her broad decks, since she must call at Buenos Ayres on her way, and at many other spots outside Uruguay and the scope of this book.

"We will therefore perform the strange feat of making a break in the trip ere it is begun. In any case, it is necessary to leave the quay over whose broad, paved surface of reclaimed land the cabs are rattling, and where the policeman and porters stand, and where, moreover, a strong group of Salvationists are singing lustily, surrounded by a motley but attentive group such as the precincts of a port attract. But the graceful *Triton* shall churn her way out into the open without us, since we will cling so far as possible to the Uruguayan shore, forging upwards through the yellowing waters, to halt at Sauce with its willow-covered lands and Colonia with its rocky beach, until Carmelo is passed, and at Nueva Palmira the River Uruguay has been fairly entered. Even then, however, it is necessary to accept the fact more or less on trust, and to confide in the accuracy of the map rather than in that of the eyesight. For the faint line that has recently appeared on the horizon to the left might as well stand for a distant streak upon the waters as for the low-lying Argentine shore that it actually represents.

"To the right, the Uruguayan bank is well defined. Here the undulations of the land swell boldly out from the edge of the river, while in many places rocks and boulders strew the sloping foreshore as though to accentuate the frontier between stream and land that is so faintly defined upon the opposite coast. Here and there the verdure of the hills is broken by the darker green bands of the eucalyptus plantations, through which from time to time gleam the white walls of an estancia-house. At intervals the chimneys of a saladero prick upwards from the nearer neighbourhood of the bank. About these centres of their doom the speck-like figures of the cattle dot the surrounding pastures, grazing in fortunate ignorance of their end.

"The traffic upon the river itself is by no means inconsiderable. Native topsail schooners laden with jerked beef, fruit and timber come gliding serenely down the stream beneath their spread of sail. One of these craft is especially indicative of the main industry of the land. The vessel is laden as high as the booms will permit with horns of cattle, the bleaching mounds of which must represent the sacrifice of many thousands of animals. There are smart Government tugs, too, that hold the official guardians of the mighty stream, and great dredgers of queer and monstrous shape that steam slowly along to find an anchorage where the bottom is shallow, and there remorselessly to bite out mouthfuls from the unduly lofty bed.

"At rarer intervals appear the ocean-going craft and sailing vessels. It would be safe to wager that there is not one of those passing downstream that is not laden with some portions or other of the bodies bequeathed to humanity by the unconsulted yet generous bovine souls. Nevertheless, the exact species of cargo would be more difficult to predict. It might be beef itself, or hides that will make leather upon which to sit while consuming the meat, or horns which will provide handles for the necessary complement of knives, or indeed many other products useful for similar purposes. There never was such a creature as the ox for the provision of a variety of articles that all eloquently urge the benefit of his death!

"A tall and majestic structure has come into sight from round a bend in the stream now, and is sweeping rapidly downwards. With grey hull, white upper-works about her rows of decks, and twin black funnels to cap the whole, she is one of the proud fleet of steamers that ply throughout the entire system of the great rivers. If the vessel upon which you may be found bears a corresponding **M** upon its funnel—which in the case of a passenger craft may be taken as a practical certainty—you may be assured that you will not be passed without recognition, even if sheltered by a mere paltry stern-wheeler that is bound for one of the small tributary streams. Combining affability with size, the whale will blow out three deep roars of salute from its great horn, that will be echoed by a like number of shrill notes from the treble whistle of the minnow. Such is the etiquette throughout the entire length of the rivers. The six blows are sounding throughout the day from the Tropics of Brazil downwards to where the La Plata and the ocean meet.

"Upon the right-hand side Fray Bentos has come into view, marked in the first place by a great collection of tall black chimneys glistening in the sun. Beneath is verdure and massive white buildings and streets of dwelling-houses, while to the front is the Lemco port with a small forest of masts rising from its waters. The place, in a double sense, represents the very incarnation of Uruguay's trade. A greedy spot that swallows live cattle by tens of thousands to render them up again in the pathetically diminished form of extract! Even now the odour of soup floats heavily in the air from across a mile of water—a proof that Fray Bentos is busily occupied in turning out its brown rivers of fluid.

"The factory, the most notable in the country, is indeed strongly symbolical of the land where starvation in ordinary circumstances of peace has never yet been known. Havana may be the paradise of the smoker, Epernay that of the champagne lover; but the eater's heaven is undoubtedly situated in Uruguay, a paradise in which the spirits of departed and honest butchers might well revel in perfect joy.

"Just above Fray Bentos the islands dot the river more plentifully than in almost any other part of the great stream. As is the case on the Paraná, it is difficult enough at times to distinguish between these and the true bank on the Argentine shore; both are equally lowly and each covered with the same density of willows and native scrub. Amongst these larger islands, however, whose surface may comprise several square miles, are numerous smaller pieces of land, and some quite diminutive specimens that can lay claim to no more than a few yards of area. These are baby islands—young territories that have only just succeeded in raising their heads above water. For an island here is conceived, grows and dies in a fashion that is vegetable rather than purely earthy. The fact is not really curious, seeing that vegetation is directly concerned in their birth.

"The conception of one of these is evident even now. A tangle of the thick leaves of the camelota—the water plant with its mauve hyacinth-like flower—has in its downward floating course fouled the earth of a shallow in midstream. The arrested clump of green has already inveigled other objects to keep it company in its trap. A few sticks and branches and tufts of grass are already fast in the embrace of the powerful stems and green leaves, while at the end that faces the stream the water-driven sand has risen at the obstacle, and has shyly protruded a small round hump or two above the ripples. The life of the thing is as uncertain as that of a seedling or of a human child. Under favourable conditions it will grow and solidify year by year until from the few leaves and sticks will have extended some square miles of tree-covered soil. On the other hand, it may be swept remorselessly away in its earliest days ere the tentative formation has had time to secure sufficiently firm hold of the earth.

"In any case the life of these islands is comparatively short, and fresh floods and currents are forming some and destroying others all the while. During these periods of flood many of them would seem possessed of the characteristics of icebergs. Detached by the irresistible force of the currents, great fragments of the vegetation and camelota-plant that cling to their sides go swirling down the stream. Though they can boast no polar bears, they are occasionally freighted with other beasts whose neighbourhood is equally undesirable. On such occasions snakes and many four-footed specimens of northern creatures form the unwilling tenants of these frail rafts of vegetation. It is said that many years ago one of unusually large size struck the shore of Montevideo itself, disgorging four jaguars, who entered the town as much to their own terror as to that of the inhabitants.

"With Fray Bentos once left in the rear, the river becomes distinctly narrowed, and, where no islands intervene, the features of either bank begin to be clearly distinguished at the same time. The Argentine shore has broken away from its dead level now, and is rising in gentle undulations; the Uruguayan coast, too, as though in a determined endeavour to retain its physical superiority, has taken to heap itself in far loftier and more imposing hills than before.

"The next town of importance at which the steamer halts is that of Paysandú, the great centre of ox-tongues. Indeed, were one to adopt the popular figurative methods of certain magazines, amazing results might well be extracted from the commerce of the place. Thus, supposing a year's accumulation of Paysandú ox-tongues were able jointly to give forth the notes that they were wont to render in life, the effect of the combined roar would probably be to deafen the entire populace of the Republic, and to blow every atom of water from the river! The number of men they would feed, and the distance they would cover if extended in a line I do not know; but it may be taken for granted that the export of these preserved instruments of bovine speech is very considerable.

"Paysandú ranks as the second commercial city in the Republic. It is true that, so far as size is concerned, it is altogether dwarfed by Montevideo, since the inhabitants of the smaller town number only twenty thousand or so. Yet, the centre of a rich pastoral and agricultural province, the place is of no little commercial importance, and, although its architecture remains largely of the pleasant but old-fashioned Spanish style, not a few new buildings and boulevards have already sprung into existence. Like the majority of towns of its kind, it is well equipped with electric lighting, telephones and other such modern appliances, although its tramcar traction is still effected by the humbler methods of the horse.

"To the north of Paysandú the stream narrows, the islands become few and far between, and the course of the river is distinct and well-defined. The landscape, too, is more varied now than that of the lower reaches. Among the Uruguayan rounded hills, a few well-marked tablelands spread their broad, level surfaces in the way that is characteristic of so many parts of the Republic. Both the inland valleys and river banks are covered with an added density of vegetation, while beaches of shining white sand jut out at intervals from the shore. As for the Argentine bank, it has quite suddenly assumed a marked individuality of its own. It is covered with a reddish yellow rolling soil, tinged only lightly with green, from which close groves of palm-trees sprout upwards for mile after mile. It is as though a portion of Africa on the one shore were facing a rather wooded and broken portion of the South Downs on the other!

"The water itself has been growing more limpid all the while, now that the dead-flat, soft alluvial soil of the Argentine bank has given way to a harder and more stony surface. It has become shallow in parts, too, and the nose of the steamer often gives a tentative turn to the right or left as she cautiously feels her way. The craft has penetrated almost to the limits of the lower stretch of the great river now, and the rising bed is a premonitory symptom of the end.

"On the right has now risen the loftiest bluff that has yet marked the Uruguayan shore. It forms one of the walls of a striking and bold tableland. The place is now known as the *Mesa de Artigas*—the table of Artigas. It was upon the summit of this hill that the Uruguayan national hero had his chief encampment, and it has been described as a desolate and lonely spot, haunted by murdered spirits and by the memory of horrors, that no living being cared to approach. The description cannot be said to hold good at the present moment. The green slopes are dotted with grazing cattle and sheep, while at one point the distant figures of two mounted Gauchos are careering to and fro, and the cattle in the neighbourhood are wheeling together and lumbering forward as a result of their manœuvres."[36]

Uruguay is known as the Oriental Republic, from its position on the eastern side of the river—the *Banda Oriental*—and it was formerly part of Argentina, but became separated in 1828, after revolutionary war, brought to an end through the mediation of Great Britain, which declared it a free and independent State.

The towns of Paysandú and Salto, which the steamer reaches on the Uruguay River, are at the head of low-water navigation. Paysandú has its tale of political savagery to tell, when its gallant defender, Leandro Gomez and his companions, were butchered in cold blood, after bombardment of the place by Brazilian forces. It has suffered much from revolution.

Both these towns are famous for the exports from their *saladeros*, or meat-curing establishments. Beyond Salto lies a rich grazing country, on whose undulating hills fat herds of cattle subsist. And indeed we are here in some of the richest stock-raising land of South America, bordering on similar districts in Southern Brazil, whose frontier lies not far to the north. Both towns are laid out with modern conveniences and public institutions. Between them navigation has its risks from rocks and shoals, and above Salto continuous navigation is not possible, as before remarked.

The Uruguay River forms in its higher reaches the eastern boundary of the Misionès province, a curious enclave belonging to Argentina, thrust in between Paraguay and Brazil; a region of sad memories, perpetuated in its name and in the lifeless villages along the banks of the Paraná and Uruguay Rivers. It was the land of the Missions of the Jesuit fathers, with their terrible and melancholy history, at which we shall presently cast a glance. First, however, we must do justice to the great land of Argentina.

CHAPTER XIV
THE RIVER PLATE AND THE PAMPAS
ARGENTINA, URUGUAY AND PARAGUAY

Of comparatively recent times there has arisen, in the temperate zone of South America, facing upon the Atlantic seaboard, a city which has rapidly become a centre of great wealth and an emporium of world trade, with a population greater than that of any other metropolis of Latin America, and with an ebb and flow of modern life and activity such as we have been prone to associate with the Anglo-Saxon rather than the Spanish development of American civilization.

Such is this city of Buenos Ayres, which we now approach; the capital of the huge territory of the Republic of Argentina, which, having its northern boundary above the Tropic of Capricorn, extends for two thousand miles towards the frigid region above Cape Horn.

It is with no feelings of envy that we call to mind the fact that this enormous and potential region might have formed part of the British Empire; a Canada in South America. For such might have been its destiny if General Beresford, in 1806, had not been forced to surrender, after obtaining possession of Buenos Ayres, and if General Whitelocke, later, had not been forced to capitulate before the organized opposition of the colonists, when Spain and France were pitted against Great Britain.

The Republic of Argentina is a country so enormous and diversified that to attempt here to give anything but the merest descriptive outlines would be futile. But let us endeavour to obtain at least a slight idea of its form and configuration.

We shall bear in mind that the country consists broadly of four topographical divisions. First is the land of the Pampas, at which we have already glanced. Second we may speak of the great plains and broken, and in part forested, deserts, of what is termed the Gran Chaco, forming that curious northern, undeveloped part of Argentina, bounded by Paraguay on the one hand and the Bolivian Andes on the other. Third we have the broken Andine region, abutting upon Bolivia and running south to the frontiers of Chile. Fourth is the vast territory of Patagonia, with the Chilean Andes on its west; a region occupying all the great narrowing part of the continent to the frigid south.

Argentina, as it is known to travel, commerce and history, is the Argentina of the Pampa. Herein lies its civilization, its great towns, its railway network, the things by which it lives.

The Pampa is a vast storehouse of food, and in some respects it does not lack beauty. Much of it is a dead level, but it has its elevations (both materially and metaphorically). It has, too, its great scourges of Nature, in the droughts which at times have ruined its industries, and which must inevitably have their periods of visitation; in the other plagues, as of the devastating locust, for which doubtless science will produce remedy or extirpation. The tempestuous winds which blow across it are at times another scourge, and the dust storms may often cause the dweller to ask whether the plagues of Egypt shall still be visited upon it! As to the droughts, we do not know if these are not extending, just as it may be that the snowfields of the Andes are diminishing, as if threatening some slow drying-up of the fountains of heaven here.

The early folk of these great plains were not of a meek and humble character, such as the Spaniards so often encountered. They were *Indios bravos*; fighters and stubborn savages, implacably hostile. Nevertheless, they gave way in time, as destiny had decreed they should.

THE PAMPAS, ARGENTINA.

Vol. II. To face p. 204.

Perhaps the things of the animal world, in its commercial sense, might be taken as most remarkable here. From few mares and stallions brought in by the men of Spain, vast equine droves, half wild, appeared with marvellous rapidity, and the later breeds multiplied similarly. It was a horseless land before the white man came. To-day a horseman pursuing his way over the vast plain is a very prominent object against the skyline. There was no ox or cow, but to-day the teeming herds in their millions—though not unnumbered—have built, through commerce, through the products of their hides and bodies, the palaces and boulevards of Buenos Ayres and its sister cities, the homes of the millionaires of this new American nation; a land where the progenitors of both man and beast first humbly crossed from old Europe, and now pour forth their riches thereto.

How far this wealth shall still increase we do not know. It may be that the limit of the pastoral industry in the Argentine Pampas has been reached or approached. The herds do not now greatly increase, since their census in 1908, of nearly thirty million head of cattle. Nature and man both take a heavy toll, the one in adverse climatic conditions, the other in waste and carelessness, as if the prodigality of the fruits of the earth were inexhaustible. On the great ranges, the cattle exist almost automatically, bearing the scorching sun or piercing wind; and in the droughts, as we pass thereover, the vision will be shocked by a lamentable spectacle of dying or rotting cattle on every hand. They are too numerous; they cannot be fed or watered, or buried when they succumb. Dust, flies and mummified bodies around offend the traveller here, and it is doubtful if man has a right to bring to being animals in such profusion that Nature cannot support them.

Possibly, in the future, better quality and lesser quantity will be the methods forced upon the cattle owners here. There is, too, a tendency towards smaller cattle ranges and perhaps more "intensive" methods, and what may be called "cattle feudalism" may beneficially suffer some modification. Irrigation, again, brings about a more varied production.

Cold storage and the making of meat extracts are, of course, one of the primary features of the cattle industry.

The enormous wheat-plains are the next source of wealth here, and other lands have cause to be grateful for both the wheat and the meat of Argentina. But the yield is comparatively low, being but twelve to thirteen bushels to the acre, for methods of cultivation are often crude.

The Argentine farmer is greatly dependent upon his wheat and maize, and if his cereal crop fails he has few resources to tide him over the bad time. The resources of Argentina in cereals are very great, and it has been calculated that there are 175 million acres of land available for their cultivation. Argentina provides a great part of the world's supply of maize, perhaps half, but in times of drought this falls very seriously.

THE CITY OF CORDOBA, ARGENTINA.

Vol. II. To face p. 206.

Social conditions on the Pampa will doubtless become modified in the future. There is too great a contrast—for a democratic or republican country—in the palatial home of the rich *estanciero* and those of the labourer. Again, the arriving immigrant, upon whom Argentina is so much dependent for labour, being unable often to obtain land for himself in this enormous country, emigrates again, and during some years half of their numbers go away elsewhere. It would seem that the Government is awake to this condition, although the remedy is slow.

The great plains of the Chaco may, in the future, bring to being another important branch of agriculture, in the growing of cotton, an industry already successfully implanted in this often fertile belt, whose rich black soils have been likened to those of the Mississippi Valley. This region might add much to the world's wealth in cotton production, but here again the question of labour is paramount.

But let us take our further way across these oceans of the Pampa, until the far line of the Andes rises on our horizon.

We may leave Buenos Ayres early and reach Rosario in the afternoon, the train making its way over a country flat as a table, with fields of wheat or maize, or pasture lands; with here and there a white-washed house and a few trees around it: trees of that variety which the all-devouring locust will not attack, for such a species there is. Perhaps the locusts are upon us, swarming in at the window of the carriage, where the native traveller crushes them vindictively. They may be as thick in the air as the flakes of a snowstorm.

On the farms, one method of getting rid of the locusts is by creating an infernal din by the beating of pots and pans, when they retreat to the lands of a neighbor! Where do they come from? The Gran Chaco has been accused of being their breeding-ground and point of departure, but whatever their origin, they are a veritable destructive plague, destroying perhaps in a few hours wide areas of smiling crops and fruitful gardens.

We reach Mendoza, beautifully situated, and watered by streams which flow from the Andes, giving life to many a fruitful sugar-cane plantation and vineyard, where under irrigation scientifically practised, from dams and conduits, the fertile soil yields up wealth in its most delightful forms, wealth of sugar, of wine, of deep pastures of alfalfa. Here, indeed, is the California of Argentina, on the slopes of the Andes, with Mendoza as its pleasing metropolis.

To the north lies Tucuman, famous in still greater degree for its production of sugar, with over thirty factories making sugar and alcohol, and yielding great wealth to their owners.

Here, however, if we are disposed to be critical, we shall point to the unlovely barracks of the labourers who are instrumental in producing this wealth. In Argentina, unfortunately, agricultural labour is little protected by the law, and contrasts are often painful. However, the climate at least is kind.

Leaving this region we shall traverse belts of dusty wilderness, which constitute part of Argentina—deserts that extend to the Andes. In this, the *Arabia Deserta* of South America, caravans in olden times, in the Colonial period, often perished and left no trace. The thirst, the dust, the savage Indian, swallowed them up. Spain ordered that all trade should pass this way, through Tucuman and Salta, the route from Peru. It was in the town hall of Tucuman town that Independence from Spain was first pronounced.

The railway system in this part of South America pushes its conquering path westwards, and through Jujuy—a name of difficult pronunciation for the uninitiated[37]—and beyond we may reach the railways of Bolivia, and so the Andes.

But the great thoroughfare of travel is the Trans-Andine Railway, a monumental work of the engineer, which, after many delays, pierced the Andes and gave means of access to Chile and the Pacific coast. We may have reached Rosario by the great highway of the river. The city is the outlet to a rich productive region, and stands on the eastern margin of the great Pampas. Rosario is, in the main, a commercial centre, whence many products of Northern Argentina are embarked on the full-flowing Paraná which washes its quays. Sacks of wheat, bales of hay, cattle and all their products, bags of sugar, maize in large quantities, and *quebracho* extract, are the principal of these exports. It reflects, or indeed in part gives rise to, the activities of Buenos Ayres, to which it comes second in importance as regards size and commerce.

Upon the site of Rosario, until the middle of last century, but a small village stood, founded in 1730, where now the straight cross-streets, in chess-board regularity, of the modern town are laid out, together with a handsome boulevard lined with residences, pleasingly interspersed with turf and trees, and many public buildings.

Paraná, which we reach in our further voyage upstream, is also classed as a seaport, notwithstanding that it is more than 600 miles from the open sea. Yonder ferry boats gives access to Santa Fé, on the opposite side of the river, a town of more ancient character, founded by the Spanish in 1573 as a halting-place on the voyage to Asuncion.

Paraná stands well above and some distance from the river, and is the capital of the rich province of Entre Rios, over whose territory the agriculturist or economist may well cast a satisfactory glance. The name of this province in English signifies "between the rivers"; descriptive of the region bounded on the one side by the waterway we have ascended, and on the other by the Uruguay River. This is the "Mesopotamia" of Argentina, otherwise known as the "garden of Argentina," from its well-watered and fertile nature, its pastoral and agricultural occupations, its products of fruits and corn, its woods and its mild and healthy climate. Had this province devoted more energy to its better development materially and morally, and less to political conflict and revolutionary strife, its picturesque designation would be more amply justified, but it has ever been one of the most turbulent districts in the Argentine confederation. Now, its prosperity has resulted in more settled conditions.

IGUAZU FALLS.

Vol. II. To face p. 210.

Our way now lies still farther up this great waterway, to the romantic land of Paraguay, for such this inland country has often been designated.

We have already seen that Asuncion is reached by steamer, and this was, indeed, until a few years ago, when the railway was built, with a train-ferry, the only means of reaching the Paraguayan capital.

> "He who can afford time for an up-river journey from Buenos Ayres to Asuncion will find the experience as instructive as anything else of the kind throughout South America. It is true that the flat pastures which go to make up the earlier stretches of the landscape lack a good deal from the picturesque point of view. But it is this very distribution of the scenery which adds to the charm of the trip, for, as the sub-tropical regions begin to exert their influence, and as the banks approach each other more nearly, the charm of the surroundings increases steadily.
>
> "After a certain point has been reached there are very few hours or dozens of miles which are not productive of some new feature or other to captivate the eye of the traveller. But not until that famous wheat centre, the Argentine town of Rosario, has been reached does this phase of the journey begin. There for the first time the flat, reed-covered banks of the river fall away, to give place to definite *barrancas*, or cliffs, that boldly mark the edge of the great stream. When the grain-shoots and line of moored steamers that mark this thriving town have been passed, the sandstone cliff continues at intervals on alternate banks; the vivid scarlet of the ceibo-tree becomes more frequent; and the clumps of camelota, the floating water hyacinth, tend to increase in size. The districts, moreover, are obeying one of the primal laws of the world in that, as the blossoms, birds and butterflies increase in brilliancy, so does the human complexion tend to grow duskier. But here this applies only to the humbler people on the banks and to the fisherfolk and watermen who sit in their crude dugout canoes. The more important persons continue white-skinned, the sole distinction between them and their brethren of the lower reaches of the river being that they now begin to form the aristocracy of the land instead of standing as the mere representatives of the wealthier classes.

"When the roofs and parks and gardens of Paraná have been passed and the buildings of Colastiné, the river port of Santa Fé, have been left behind, the warmer airs already give a foretaste of what is to come farther to the north. All this time the vegetation has been increasing on the banks. The wide stretches of open, treeless pastures have long ago fallen away. The country where the cattle graze is now pleasantly interspersed with clumps of indigenous trees, and the line of the banks is obscured in parts by dense clusters of verdure, in which the palms begin to occupy a more and more important space.

"Presently on the right bank of the river, and thus to the left of the steamer's bow, appears that curious low-lying country of the Chaco, the alternate forests, swamps and pastures that extend from here northwards through the entire length of Paraguay and well into Bolivia on the other side. There are orchids hanging up aloft among the foliage now, and doubtless a monkey or two among the denser clumps of woodland. But these pioneer creatures of the Tropics to the north are rare enough here, and in any case are invisible. Their presence thus is generally unsuspected by the newcomer, which is not the case with the mosquitoes and those clouds of other *bichos*, whose numbers increase in the most amazing fashion with almost every hour that goes by.

"Indeed, did one judge of the winged pests of these neighbourhoods by the myriads which abound above the fervid waters, the outlook would be sufficiently unpromising even to the most mosquito-hardened of men. The song of this plague is continuous of an evening now, and when the daylight has vanished in the abrupt fashion in which it is wont to fade away in these latitudes, the electric globes of the steamer are all but obscured by the insects that dance about them so thickly as to resemble dense clouds of smoke that roll in confused masses about a half-seen flame! Fortunately, these river reaches—most beloved of all the haunts of the winged creatures—do not afford a fair and moderate sample of the insect life of these latitudes, quite considerable enough though the usual run of this is wont to be.

"Arrived at the Argentine town of Corrientes, one of the most important strategic spots in the whole river system has been reached. To one bound upstream this is the parting of the river ways. A few miles to the north of the town the choice is open to the traveller whether he will turn to the right and ascend the waters of the Alto Paraná, with Argentina on his right hand and Paraguay on his left, or whether he will keep straight on to the north and reverse this territorial situation, having Argentina on his left and Paraguay on his right.

"The main line of the waters, with Asuncion as its object, lies straight to the north, and almost immediately after leaving Corrientes the steamer has entered the Paraguay River. It is at this point that the somewhat curious nomenclature of the various streams becomes most evident. It is the remarkable fate of the Paraguayan when bound from his home to the Atlantic Ocean to have to descend three different rivers, or, if you prefer it, various stretches of the same river known by three different names. From the point of view of fluvial equity, there is no doubt that considerable wrong has been done to the River Paraguay in the way of nomenclature. Why this splendid navigable stream, at its junction with the cascade-broken and far shorter Alto Paraná, should yield its name to that of the lesser current, and should continue to flow southwards as the Paraná, is a sufficiently incomprehensible matter to most geographers. And then, when it has all but run its course, the river performs a second wedding, with the Uruguay this time, and again changes its name. But on this occasion neither stream obtains the advantage over the other, for both roll their few remaining miles to the sea under the entirely fresh name of La Plata. Nevertheless, there does not seem to be a doubt that, from the point of view of importance, the name of the great stream which rises to the north of the inland Republic should be the Paraguay for its entire course as far as the ocean.

A CHACO FLOOD.

Vol. II. To face p. 214.

"This digression, however, has led us away from the upstream journey to Asuncion. Once in the Paraguay River, the beauties of the scene would seem to have become more marked. The banks have drawn sufficiently near to each other for their increasing charms to become plain. No longer does the steamer steer a tortuous course through a maze of low and reedy islands that never permit the stranger to be certain whether he is gazing on the mainland or whether further channels at the bank lie between him and the actual shore.

"Now the banks of the stream, with their flower-starred vegetation, are plainly defined. Once to the north of the mouth of the Bermejo tributary, moreover, which pours its amazingly red and muddy waters into the main stream, the river has become comparatively limpid. Alligators had already made their appearance in the Paraná; but such banks of sand and mud as emerge here and there from the waters of the Paraguay are far more thickly covered with the sluggish bodies of the small saurians, that in these latitudes seldom exceed six or seven feet.

"Presently, as the steamer drops her anchor before a port to her right, there is a significant touch of colour about the small official boat which puts out to her from the shore. Hitherto the light blue and white of Argentina has flown at the stern of these craft. But from this one for the first time floats the red, white, and blue of Paraguay. The steamer has arrived at Humaitá, the first port of the inland Republic."[38]

A massive, stark ruin, standing up on the bank of the river, the church of Humaitá, carries us into the history of the dreadful war which laid the land desolate here, and to which we must shortly refer. Continuing for the present our way upstream, the view extends over tobacco and sugar-cane fields, interspersed with luxuriant banana groves. Reed huts cluster here and there near the bank, and groups of dark-skinned workers are seen. On the opposite shore a fringe of dense vegetation hides the Chaco plains—the haunt of the savage Indian and the tapir, but marked by occasional clearings. Rafts of *quelracho* timber float down the stream, the heavy wood buoyed up by trunks of a lighter kind, for the *quelracho* does not float. Soon we reach the mouth of the Pilcomayo, with its low bank, and then the roofs and spires of Asuncion come into the field of view, the salient points of a city that spreads itself over the rolling ground, surrounded by pleasant verdure.

Asuncion is to be regarded as a picturesque city. There is a wealth of flower, which often covers the hovels on the outskirts. The city is built partly on its hills and partly on the sandy riverine plain, and contains some interesting buildings. Life here is generally simple, and has certain attractions by reason of this simplicity. It is nigh upon the tropic zone, but its environment is such that the climate is pleasant indeed, and, in fact, has been enthusiastically described by some as "containing all the elements of perfection."

Asuncion was long the seat of Spanish rule, which extended over this vast region of river and forest, and here, among other phases, the bitter struggle between the Church and the Jesuits was played out.

Life, we have said, is simple, even for the upper class, although in its way typical of Spanish American culture. In humbler circles, clothing is simple. A cotton chemise is a sufficient garment for a woman, and perhaps a white *manta* round the head, in the fashion brought by Spain from the Moors; whilst her husband wears nothing more than a loose shirt and trousers—clothing that costs little and lasts long.

These sartorial conditions refer to the Indian folk who, however, constitute the bulk of the nation. Upper-class people, of course, wear boots and shoes, and would indignantly refute any aspersion as to being backward in the refinements of life. There are some good buildings in Asuncion, showing the customary Spanish American ideas in civic architecture. The most prominent edifice is a bank, built originally as a palace by the younger Lopez, and there is a national college and a public library, but educational progress is slow in Paraguay. The principal streets are paved, and lighted with gas and electricity, and there are street cars and telephones.

The name of Lopez brings forward one of the most dreadful periods of history in this part of South America, upon which we may well pause a space.

Francisco Solano Lopez, dictator of Paraguay, and self-styled "Protector of the equilibrium of the La Plata," forced his country into war against Brazil, Uruguay and Argentina, who, aggrieved, combined for the purpose of suppressing him, "until no elements of war should be left in Paraguay," as their declaration ran. The country was invaded, the war lasted five years, 1865 to 1870; a struggle involving enormous sacrifice of blood and treasure, closing only when the Paraguayans were practically annihilated. During the struggle every male Paraguayan was forced to bear arms; there were regiments of boys from twelve to fifteen years old; women were used as beasts of burden to carry ammunition and stores, and were murdered or left to die by the wayside when their strength gave out. From a population of nearly one and a half million, that of Paraguay fell as a consequence of the struggle to a quarter of a million. It is recorded that, in the retreat, Lopez ordered every town and village to be destroyed and every living animal slaughtered. Imagining a conspiracy against his life, this half-crazed dictator, it is recorded, ordered hundreds of the foremost citizens of Paraguay to be seized and executed, including his own brother and brothers-in-law, judges, cabinet ministers, officers, bishops, two hundred foreigners and several diplomatic representatives of the legations. The end of this extraordinary specimen of a Spanish American ruler was death in the river, for, having been reduced to a handful of adherents, on the northern frontier of Paraguay, he was surprised by Brazilians, and shot, as he endeavoured to swim the stream.

Leaving these dreadful reminiscences of civilized savagery, however, let us take our way through the Republic. Much of it is extremely fertile; rich soil abounding in meadows and pastures, with such varied products as might make of this portion of the continent a veritable garden or orchard. Our eyes rest on groves of orange-trees, clustering with golden fruit, on fields of waving sugar-cane of immense growth, on vineyards and tobacco fields, on cotton and hemp plantations. So prolific are the citrus fruits that hogs are sometimes fattened on oranges. Millions of dozens of the fruit are exported down the river to the large towns on its banks.

The principal product, however, is the well-known *yerba maté*, or Paraguayan tea, and the growing and collecting of this gives occupation to the Indian peasants whom we see clustered in the fields or simple villages. The cost of production of this article is small, and, exported to Argentina, Brazil and

Chile, the leaf takes the place to some extent in those communities of tea and coffee. The leaves of the shrub, the *Ilex Paraguayensis*, are stripped, sun-dried and packed in sacks for export.

This tea could be sold in England at perhaps sixpence per pound, but, notwithstanding its useful qualities, it is almost unknown in Britain.

Paraguay is a land where soil and climate lends itself well to stock-raising, and doubtless this industry in the future will be much more extensively cultivated in the Republic, in view of the world's needs for the products it yields. Natural pasture is abundant, shelter is unnecessary, but drought at times is a source of loss. The breed of the cattle, too, calls for improvement. The great South American meat and meat-extract companies have already cast eyes on the possibilities of the Paraguayan pastures.

BRINGING HOME AND PACKING YERBA MATE.

Vol. II. To face p. 220.

If we are students of social science, we may recollect that this land we are momentarily treading was the scene of an interesting experiment in communism, when, some twenty-five years ago, William Lane and his companions, of Sydney, founded their colony of "New Australia." This little band of Australians, who at least had the courage of their convictions, suffered endless misfortunes in their endeavour to demonstrate their economic theories, in which there was to be neither master nor servant, nor rich nor poor, but each for all. Before starting, their individual possessions were made over to the common fund. The Government of Paraguay treated the enterprise exceedingly well, granted them a tract of extremely fertile land, which, however, was in a remote spot, and helped them in various ways, believing, as did the band of Australians, that success would attend their endeavours. But at length disillusionment arose, and although the leader and a few of his adherents struggled bravely on, disaster befel the settlement, which lapsed finally into purely individualistic methods.

A far earlier "socialistic" system flourished in this part of South America. The story of the Jesuit missions is one of great interest, but with a sad ending, and we may cast a glance at it here.

> "It was in 1588 that the first Jesuits arrived in Paraguay, where they met with a warm welcome at the hands of the colonists, between whom and the missionary Fathers a bitter feud was eventually destined to spring up. These early workers made a cosmopolitan company, counting among their number Spaniards, Portuguese, Italians and Scots, besides other nationalities. Setting dauntlessly out into the forests of Paraguay, they passed from tribe to tribe, making converts of the Indians in a fashion sufficiently wholesale to receive some condemnation at the hands of their detractors. However much or however little the average Guaraní may have understood of his actual reception into the Christian faith, the perils and hardships of the early missionaries remained the same, and these were undoubtedly sufficient to tax the resolution of any but the most single-hearted pioneer.
>
> "Little by little, as more Jesuits arrived from abroad to assist in the work, and as the numbers of the Guaraní converts grew, began the definite foundations of that society of the Paraguayan missions which was feared and hated by those Spaniards outside its borders who imagined, rightly or wrongly, that its presence was the cause of much material wrong to themselves. This country of the Jesuits had every right to be known as a State. It administered its own laws and authority, and was subject to none of the local colonial officials, a circumstance that undoubtedly gave rise to numerous outbursts of jealousy. It was, moreover, rigidly shut off from the outer world, and, although travellers were permitted to pass, closely watched, from one of its towns to another, none but the Jesuit administrators were in the least conversant with the affairs of the community, and with the events which were

happening in the State. It is this latter circumstance, of course, which has been responsible for so many of the disputes concerning actual facts—arguments which have arisen both during the period of the Jesuit dominion and after the expulsion of the Fathers. But in any case no dispute has ever arisen concerning the fact that this land of the Jesuits was a self-governing State, whether it be known by any of the various names which have been applied to it—a republic, an empire, or a socialistic community pure and simple.

"The mission country of the Jesuits was situated amid those delightful tracts of land where the modern Republics of Paraguay, Brazil and Uruguay now meet. From north to south it lay, roughly, between the parallels of 25° and 30°, and thus it comprised a stretch of territory the open spaces of which may rightfully be called 'the Garden of South America.' We may now survey this spot in the height of its prosperity, beginning with some aspects of its thirty towns, which, of course, include some of the most salient features of all.

"The Jesuits of Paraguay were nothing if not consistent, and their policy was eloquently shown in the construction of their towns. None of their converts, decreed the missionaries, should be permitted to outdo his, or her, neighbourhood in the matter of dress and outward appearance. The priests did their best to ensure equality and the absence of heartburning by a regulation that every Indian should be garbed exactly the same, both in material and cut, as were his brethren and sisters. This same theory was made to apply in the case of the dwelling-places of the Guaranís. It has been remarked that these resembled each other as closely as one drop of water resembles another. 'The arrangement of these,' says Alvear, who wrote from personal experience, 'is so uniform that when you have seen one you may say that you have seen them all. Some tiny freak of architecture or some little touch of private adornment—that is the only difference that may be remarked. Essentially they are all the same, and this has been brought to such a pitch that those who travel through them are apt to begin to wonder if they are not being accompanied by the same enchanted town, the eyes of a lynx being needed to tell the difference between the inhabitants and clothes of one of these places and those of another. The plan of them all is rectangular, the streets stretching from north to south and from east to west, and the Plaza, which is always roomy and level, in the middle. The church, college and cemetery occupy that side of the Plaza that faces north.'

"This description affords, at all events, a rough and general outline of one of the Jesuit towns. It leaves, however, many details of interest to be filled in. The aspect of one of these places, it may be said, was extremely pleasant, the Jesuits who understood these matters very thoroughly, having introduced orange-groves and other such growths with consummate skill among the buildings. The church would be a most solidly built edifice, containing three or five naves, as the case might be. Its interior, moreover, was richly decorated by the Indian craftsmen and workers in metal, and here, one imagines, some distinguishing originality must have occurred, although no doubt this was avoided as much as possible.

"Attached to the college, which was usually a very large building, were the workshops and storehouses of the town, which were thus under the immediate eye of the Fathers. The buildings in which the Indians themselves were accommodated were very extensive but low-roofed structures, being some sixty yards in length and ten in breadth. The majority of the buildings were contrived of great blocks of the locally found *Tacurú* stone, which for the purpose of cutting possesses the very unusual advantage of being comparatively soft when first taken from the earth, hardening little by little as it is exposed to the air. The magnificent woods of the neighbouring forests were frequently employed in addition, and the ubiquitous *adobe* was made to serve here and there. All the buildings were very solidly tiled.

"So much for the general description of one of those Jesuit towns of which only the ruins now remain, all but swallowed up by the encroaching verdure of the forest. In their neighbourhood was nearly always a stone-lined spring, welling out into a pool planted about with palms, and thus presenting a most agreeable appearance. Near this would be the chapels of the 'Stations of the Cross.'

"Finally, it must be said that many of these centres which were most exposed to the raids of the hostile Brazilian inhabitants of San Paolo were strongly fortified, being surrounded by a deep ditch and a solid wall of hardened mud.

"Each of these towns was in charge of two Jesuits, not too large a number, it must be admitted, to have control of a town the population of which was probably about four thousand. These, however, were assisted by numerous Guaraní officials, and their management appears to have been conducted with exemplary smoothness.

"Having now obtained a glimpse of the plan and aspects of a Jesuit mission town, it is time to consider some attributes that are at least as important—its inhabitants. Proceeding downwards along its hierarchy from the two Jesuit Fathers in charge—who were responsible only to a superior of their own order who travelled continually to and fro between the various towns—we arrive at the higher Guaraní officials. At the head of these was a *cacique*, who in a sense acted as Governor of the place, although his office was under the closest supervision of the two Jesuits in charge. There were also *corregidores*, *regidores*, *alcaldes*, and many other officials, whose posts corresponded more or less with those held by Spaniards in the somewhat cumbrous municipal scheme that obtained in the peninsula.

"In order that the position of these dusky dignitaries should be properly emphasized they were raised above the law which decreed perfect equality of dress for all, and on feast days their uniforms were wont to be sufficiently gorgeous to distinguish them from the rest.

"The dress of the rank and file of the inhabitants was simple to a degree. The material employed for that of both men and women was white cotton. The men wore a species of shirt above short breeches, while the women were dressed in petticoats, above which was an armless chemise known as the *typoi*. The hair was plaited into one or two tails, and was generally adorned with a crimson flower. To such a degree had this doctrine of similarity of costume become implanted into the minds of the Indians that, after the expulsion of the Jesuits, those who succeeded the missionaries—and endeavoured in vain to carry on the work—were astonished at the tenacity with which they clung to it. Desirous of rooting out entirely the influence of the Jesuits, they assiduously pointed out to the Indians the advantages of individuality in dress. But it was a very long time before one of these could bring himself to distinguish his person from the rest by means of any of those added touches which are usually so eagerly sought after by the dusky races.

"The supposition that Satan finds work for idle hands to do was acknowledged by the Jesuits with an enthusiasm on which was founded the principal tenets of their communities. In the mission towns any risk of this kind was quite infinitesimal! Indeed, one of the charges levelled by the opponents of the missionaries has been to the effect that they harnessed the Guaranís from the age of five years upwards to an endless and grinding routine of toil. Indeed, in estimating the benefits derived by the company of the Jesuits from this fount of labour, a very gifted modern Argentine writer estimates the eighteenth-century Guaraní population of the Paraguayan missions at some 150,000, adding that, so healthy was the climate of their country that almost the entire force of this community was available, invalids being almost unknown. In this he unconsciously pays a notable tribute to the methods employed in the 'Reductions'—by which name these mission towns were also known. For this remarkable lack of invalids may well be compatible with the circumstances attending ordinary hard work, but they suggest nothing of that grinding toil such as the *conquistadores* were only too frequently accustomed to inflict on the aborigines—labour involving broken health and premature death.

"The admittedly healthy condition of the Jesuitical Guaranís is in itself sufficient to refute such a charge as this.

"The various kinds of work carried on in the mission towns were of an amazingly comprehensive nature. Even their most hostile critics have never attempted to dispute the administrative abilities of the missionaries. These found a full opportunity in the fertile soil and varied products of the country. One of the first industries they took up was that of collecting the famous Paraguayan tea, the yerba maté, from the forests in which it grew. Undoubtedly this was one of the severest tasks which the Guaranís had to undertake, since the yerba-tree, the *Ilex Paraguayensis*, favours the denser forests that are the haunt of the jaguar, the venomous snake and countless noxious insects. Moreover, as the yerba maté-trees in the neighbourhood of the settlements became used up, the journeys of the Indians grew longer and more difficult, and the return marches, under the burden of the yerba loads, still more strenuous.

"Another industry which rapidly attained to great importance was that of cattle-breeding. It is difficult to picture the Jesuit Fathers galloping with flying robes after the scampering herds of cattle, gathering them into *rodeos*, and 'parting' them after the fashion of the gaucho—and this they undoubtedly did not do! At the same time, it is certain that they must have closely supervised their dusky herdsmen; for the numbers of their cattle rapidly increased to an extent which could only have been possible under an efficient, and comparatively scientific, management. This will be evident when it is explained that more than thirty thousand head of cattle grazed on one of their estates alone, and that at the time of the expulsion of the company their pastures were found to contain nearly 800,000 cattle, nearly 100,000 horses and mules, and over 200,000 sheep and goats.

"Beyond this there were the fields of cotton, maize, rice, sugar-cane, tobacco, and all those cereals which went to make up the store of the mission towns, as well as the spreading groves of orange-trees, and all the fruits of the sub-tropics and of Southern Europe which were cultivated with immense success in the rich red soil of Paraguay. It is a tribute to the energy of the Jesuits, moreover, that sufficient wheat was grown within the missions to render them self-supporting in this respect, when the small amount of wheat is taken into consideration that is at present produced within the Republic of Paraguay.

"It was in these pastoral and agricultural pursuits that the main supply of Guaraní labour was employed. The Jesuits saw to it that the tasks of the Indians were made as attractive as possible. Thus they would march to the fields singing chants and preceded by a small band of instruments, and they would return in the same impressive fashion when the labours of the day were done. In all such ways as this the work of the Indians was lightened, and undoubtedly the policy possessed its practical side in that far more satisfactory agricultural results were obtained from these contented people than would have been the case had they been dejected and apathetic.

"The scope of the mission work, however, was by no means confined to the pastoral and agricultural pursuits. The community was entirely self-supporting, and it was thus necessary to quarry the stone of which the town buildings were constructed, to build the small vessels in which much of the produce was sent to be sold in the large cities lower down the river, and even to found the cannons and to produce the gunpowder which were necessary in order to defend the settlements from the slave-raiding attacks of those arch-enemies of the missions, the *Mamelucos*, who came out with fire and sword from the Brazilian town of San Paolo.

"But, when the disposition and attainments of the original Guaraní tribe are taken into consideration, some of the most remarkable achievements of the missionaries were in connection with the finer arts and crafts rather than with the cruder labours of the main industries. It is true that at the head of each of these branches was a Jesuit who was a complete master of his particular art or craft. But this alone does not suffice to explain the astonishing progress made in these directions by a race that a generation or two before had represented one of the most primitive types of Indian in the world—naked savages without the faculty of hieroglyphics, unable to count beyond the few first numbers, ignorant of the very rudiments of music, and lacking sufficient imagination to provide themselves even with a reasonable supply of that superstition which stands for the religion of the savage.

"Yet it was from these very folk that were produced craftsmen of a really able type. It was they who, under the coaching of the missionaries, learned to become carpenters, to carve stone with professional cunning, and who became expert locksmiths, gunsmiths and workers in metals. There were many weavers and printers, and among them were a certain number who had actually attained to the expert art of watchmaking. Among the most astonishing walks of life, however, to which the Guaraní was transported was that of painter—in the artistic sense of the vocation. Hand in hand with this art went that of music. Indeed, one of the proofs of how thoroughly these matters were undertaken lies in the fact of the bringing over from Europe with a view to teaching the Guaranís music and singing, of Padre Juan Basco, who had previously been at the head of an archducal institution of music.

"A school and a hospital were attached to each Reduction, and each of these, in addition, was provided with an asylum for the aged and infirm. Even here a certain amount of work was carried on, and the inmates of this institution were given such light tasks as they could perform."[39]

This colonization system was broken up by the *Mamelucos*, the greedy folk of San Paolo, who, having enslaved the Indians of that part of Brazil, cast envious eyes upon the peaceful labour of the missions, which they longed to impress in their own services. They therefore began a series of merciless onslaughts on the settlements, which, however, valiantly defended themselves for a time. But the Arcadia was doomed to fall, and the Jesuits were expelled from Paraguay in 1768, and little remains now but the ruin of their wonderful work, which Nature rapidly covered up with her generous robes of flower and foliage, as if desirous of hiding from view the brutalities of mankind in this one of her fairest provinces of South America.

We shall now leave this fertile heart of the continent, to traverse with rapid strides a region of a very different nature: that of the "Far South"—a south, however, whose attributes of climate and general environment are not such as we generally associate with that point of the compass, and of which we have obtained a passing glimpse in our survey of the great Cordillera.

In the southern-most part of the New World, the tapering portion of the South American continent, lies a vast region of which comparatively little is heard or known, yet one which in the future must take its place in the economic development of the globe. This is the Territory extending throughout the lower portion of Argentina, Patagonia and Tierra del Fuego.

It is a land lying far beyond the Tropics, in part a sort of Siberia of South America, terminating in those regions which Magellan described as "stark with eternal cold."

We generally speak of Argentina and Chile as if they were compact topographical and political entities, instead of territories between two and three thousand miles long, covering zones on the surface of the globe comparable, as far as latitude is concerned, to one extending from nigh mid-Africa, through Europe into Scotland, with climate similarly varying.

But this southern land has great possibilities. It has received a bad name, largely resulting upon the description of Darwin, who visited it in the voyage of the *Beagle*, a reputation which more recent travellers have shown not to be deserved. Darwin spoke of the "curse of sterility" and of the eternally "dreary landscape," but, like Siberia, Patagonia may prove to be a region desirable in many respects.

Yet Patagonia strikes the traveller as huge and elemental, and settlement and development, as far as they go, are but the work of the few recent years. It offers great and abrupt contrasts of pampa and mountain, with rivers cutting across the plains from the Andes to the Atlantic.

> "On the Atlantic coastline it is four or five days' ride to the nearest farm. In the interior Nature enfolds you with her large, loose grasp. Who, having once seen them, can forget the Pampas? Evening, and the sun sloping over the edge of the plain like an angry eye, an inky-blue mirage half blotting it out; in the middle distance grass rolling like an ocean to the horizon, lean thorn, and a mighty roaring wind. This wild land, ribbed and spined by one of the greatest mountain chains in the world, appears to have been the last habitation of the great beasts of the older ages. It is now the last country of all to receive man, or rather its due share of human population. Out there in the heart of the country one seems to stand alone, with nothing nearer or more palpable than the wind, the fierce mirages, and the limitless distances."[40]

However, farms and cattle ranges are springing up, and Nature has placed in one spot on the coast an important petroleum field, to say nothing of the valuable forests.

This far southern region of South America is shared by the British Empire, in its distant outpost of the Falkland Isles, forming its most southerly colony. The latitude here in the south corresponds roughly to that of

England in the north, but climate is very different, with a constantly overcast and rainy sky, although the extremes of heat and cold are far less. The treeless, grass-covered lands maintain large numbers of sheep. The little capital of Stanley is mainly built of wood, with a Government House of grey stone, calling to mind an Orkney or Shetland manse. There is nothing of Spanish American atmosphere here. Far from the mainland, the only association with the continent of South America of the Falkland Isles is that they are the headquarters of the bishop of that diocese, which, as we have seen elsewhere, covers so wide a field in Spanish America, and perhaps the fact that Argentina still regards the possession of these somewhat melancholy and remote sea-girt isles by Britain with disapproval; claiming them as hers. The name is immortal in the destruction of the German fleet in those waters during the Great War.

CHAPTER XV
TRADE AND FINANCE

There is a certain element of interest, apart from money-making, attaching to commerce with that wide and varied group of peoples which come under the distinctive nomenclature of the Latin American Republics, and this is perhaps a fortunate circumstance. There is, as already remarked, an element of adventure about trade operations therewith which may be said to stimulate and assist enterprise—the enterprise of buying and selling in those remote and still half-developed communities.

Your merchant packs and dispatches his wares, marking his packages with names and destinations whose lettering and pronunciation, though they may cost him an effort to write or speak correctly, have in them something redolent of the blue seas and skies of the Tropics, upon whose shores they will presently be landed, to be handed over—the attentions of cigarette-smoking and gold-laced Customs officers satisfied amid much Castilian *chárla*—to the mercies in many cases of rude but patient muleteers, when, bound on the backs of mules they will be borne over mountain paths and through tangled jungles to many a distant interior village of the Pampas or the Cordillera.

And those returning goods which lie upon our quays, fresh from the hold of the steamer which brought them hither, have their own origin stamped upon them, and often betray by their aroma their special nature. Who has not walked upon the docks and remarked with interest the bales of coffee, the piles of hides, the sacks of ore, the packages of raw cocoa and other raw material sent hither, the product of industrious natives of the picturesque *hacienda* and the mine?

Your commercial traveller, too, if he be a man of parts—and such he must be to treat successfully in these communities—smells the battle from afar, and, setting forth again, girds himself thereto, prepared to exercise that needful show of courtesy which even commercial dealings require in those lands where Spanish and Portuguese is the medium of barter or sale, and schools his tongue to speak in their softer accents.

The trade of Latin America is now a much coveted field. The English merchant, who long held this field, has now to contend with the keen competition of others. There was, before the war, the German, who by ability and craft had firmly and remuneratively established himself therein, and who now seeks to build up the trade edifice which the punishment of his criminal war has caused to fall. There is the American, as keen as any, studying by what means he may overcome the disadvantages which worked against his more successful exploitation of the Latin American sphere in the past, and thinking, perhaps, to predominate over his rivals. There are the French, the Italian, the Spaniard and others, all demanding their share; and coming forward now is the Japanese, acclaiming his right to whatever he may wrest, either from the sphere of his competitors or in the finding of fresh pastures.

From whence is this keen desire to profit by the trade of the Central and South American States? Despite its attendant risks, of distance, of long credits, of "slow payers" and repudiated debts, it must be profitable. There must be a demand for goods, a wide and sufficient market and a margin of considerable balance over costs and expenses.

This is, in fact, the case; but as we shall note, it is possible to overdraw these attractions of the counting-house and the manufactory.

Latin America is a territory whose wealth and population are growing. There is an increasing class demanding the things of luxury and necessity which Europe and North America produce, and which Japan produces—for it will be unwise to leave these sharp-witted traders of Asia out of our survey. The Latin American peoples are plastic and emotional, imitative, pleasure-loving, fond of personal adornment. They are emerging from the poverty and austerity of the influence of the Colonial period. Some of them are very wealthy. Their women must be clad in expensive finery; their homes must be furnished with showy furniture; upon their tables must lie the delicacies that other nations enjoy.

So far they have not learned to exercise the ingenuity latent within them to make these things—although here is a factor we shall shortly consider—for themselves, and, in consequence, a stream of articles,—textiles, machinery, clothing, prepared foodstuffs, jewellery, furniture and all else—takes its way from foreign ports towards their shores.

It is part of our task here to consider what are the conditions of successful trading in these growing communities, but before doing so it will be well to sound a note of caution as to over-exaggerated expectations of trade and profits in Latin America.

In the first place an unlimited market for exported articles of luxury and need argues a considerable class of persons capable of absorbing such.

Compared with other communities, the purchasing class of Latin America cannot be regarded as very extensive. We have here a score of States or Republics whose total population perhaps approximates eighty million souls, all but a small proportion of whom, probably less than ten per cent., are folk of the poorest class, without purchasing power for more than the barest necessities or simplest articles of everyday life—articles which they themselves can produce—the great bulk of them illiterate Indians or Mestizos. Until the standard of life of these people be raised very considerably—and there is little evidence of this uplifting so far—they cannot develop either the power or the inclination to spend. Their masters—like masters all the world over—pay them the lowest possible wage, blind to the economic fact that this parsimony rebounds upon themselves, stinting production, output, consumption and demand.

Thus it is that the purchasing power of the Latin American population is a limited one, and markets and warehouses may readily be over-stocked, stuffed—as has happened on various occasions—with goods which cannot be sold, or must be sold at a loss.

Especially is this the case with articles of textile manufacture, bales of cloth, dress fabrics and so forth, when all the large emporiums and shops have had their shelves loaded and could digest no more. All the merchants of Spanish American capitals and large towns have experienced this, and although the cessation of imports during the war emptied the shelves and disorganized their markets, it cannot be long, given the keen desire to forward goods from abroad, when the same plethora will recur.

There is a further condition to consider, of still greater economic importance.

The tendency of nations in the future is bound to become more and more self-supplying in the manufacture or production of articles of everyday consumption. The spread of knowledge, the need for local employment, the high cost of production and—a very important matter—the high cost of carriage or transport, which latter, in fact, is becoming prohibitive in some cases, are all factors making towards the principle of self-supply.

As an economic principle, this of self-supply is altogether sound, and its extension to the utmost is advisable and beneficial. It will help to eliminate waste; it will perhaps work against over-production and over-competition, both wasteful forces; it will tend to conserve the native resources of the globe, especially in fuel and raw material, which, during the "factory age," have been severely drawn upon and in many instances ruthlessly wasted. To produce a thing where it is to be consumed, we may repeat, rather than carrying it over seas and continents from distant producer to consumer, is a sound economic and sociological principle, so far little recognised.

The growth of such conditions, however, is not likely to be of benefit to trade in general. One of the first branches of manufacture to be affected thereby is the textile industry of Britain and other lands as regards the export trade. It has been shown in these pages that the Latin American countries, in some instances, have now set up their own mills and are manufacturing their own textiles. This is specially true of such countries as Brazil, Mexico, Argentina and others, where the production of "piece goods" and other textiles and articles of clothing is being extensively carried out with marked success, and with a corresponding limitation of import. These mills are often worked by water-power, and so are free from the difficult and expensive element of fuel. Labour, moreover, is much cheaper, even if less efficient, than abroad.

The same condition is growing as regards other manufactured articles, and there is no physical reason why the whole of the Latin American States should not manufacture many articles for their own requirements which at present they import. They possess within their own shores all the necessary raw material, except in some few instances.

But do they possess the skill to make these articles? There is little doubt that the Latin American folk, the artisan, the mechanic, the craftsman, are learning the methods of manufacture in many fields. They may not be an inventive folk, but they are an imitative folk, and possessed withal of great patience and painstaking ingenuity.

These last-named qualities are revealed in their ancient native industries. Any one who takes the trouble to examine the examples of these old crafts will often be struck by their beauty and ingenuity. In textile work they excelled. The old tapestries of the Inca and the fabrics of the Aztec, and of the Queches of Guatemala, of the Mayas, and, in brief, all others of the cultured or semi-cultured early folk of Spanish America reveal this, and examples are to be seen in the museums. The Indians of the Andes to-day make their own "tweeds" of sheep or llama wool; also their own felt hats. They weave ponchos of Alpaca wool that are waterproof, so closely are they hand-woven. They dyed these things in beautiful native patterns (often of much archæological interest) with native dyes which in some cases were superior to the imported synthetic dyes of Europe. As a matter of fact, it is unfortunate from a true economic and artistic point of view that these native industries should be displaced by outside products.

Again, such articles as the Panama hat of Ecuador and Colombia show of what the Indian is capable; as did the beautiful jewellery, in precious metals and stones, of the ancient culture-area of Central America, or the exquisite vessels and objects of adornment of the Incas, some of which still exist. The powers in stone-working are seen by the remarkable structures scattered over the whole Spanish American world, revealing the use of the chisel.

There is, however, no need here to labour this argument, but it is more than possible that a marked growth of Latin American craftsmanship will come to being again, under the stimulus of modern needs.

On the other hand, it is not to be supposed that the foreign manufacturer is likely immediately to find the ground cut away from under his feet. There are numerous articles of commerce which the Latin American folk do not, and possibly cannot, make for themselves, or not yet.

Among these matters is the important one of machinery. So far, throughout the length and breadth of the Latin American States, not a single locomotive has ever had its birth, and that in a land where the locomotive is so essential a factor. Nor is bar iron or steel rail rolled anywhere here (except possibly a little experimental work in Mexico and elsewhere). In fact, the manipulation of iron and steel has not yet come to being.

When we take note of the mines to be worked, the cotton, sugar and other mills and factories to be equipped, the railways to be built and maintained, the demand for motor-cars, the call for agricultural machinery, the use of household utensils of iron and steel, the wire fencing and a host of articles, it is evident that the field of trade here will not yet be cut off.

In the superior textile again, skill has not yet reached a capacity to supply all wants. The growing requirements of people to be clothed by the best class of goods will doubtless long keep up the imports of such, unless governments institute absolutely prohibitive tariffs—a matter upon which it is impossible to speculate.

It would be out of our province here to deal in detail with the various articles of trade in the Latin American field. There are recent sources of such information which fill all requirements.[41]

There is an important condition in connection with the conduct of business in Spanish America. This is, in the more leisurely and courteous bearing observed in such transactions, and the commercial traveller or his chief is well advised to study it.

The merchant or business man here will not be hustled or too brutally—in a commercial sense—approached. A friendly chat, inquiries as to matters of mutual interest, or upon current events, or regarding the members of each other's family, or other subjects general or politely personal, paves the way to the more concrete business of the occasion.

"Personality" counts for much in Spanish American relations, not only in society but in business. The Spanish-speaking people have a word for which in English we have no exact equivalent; that is the word, or adjective, *simpatico* (or the feminine form *simpatica*). It does not necessarily mean exactly "sympathetic" or "personal magnetism"—to use the latter rather stupid English term. It means intuitive, comprehensive. A person who is *simpatico* may command much greater attention than one who is not.

It is to be recollected that the Latin American man of any position is, or aims at being, a *caballero*, a gentleman, and it is to be remarked that this is a pleasing and valuable ideal, which might well be more closely cultivated amid the often boorish methods of Anglo-Saxondom.

Thus your commercial traveller should accept the proffered cigar or cigarette—there is generally such an offer—of his desired client, or offer one himself, and not attempt to come immediately to the point or instantly thrust his wares beneath the nose of the person upon whom he calls, hoping to make an immediate sale and rush out to perform the same operation on perhaps a rival dealer next door.

That "Time is money" has also its rendering in Spanish: *Tiempo es oro*, and it does not follow that business will be delayed by diplomatic methods. Yet this habit of courtesy should not merely be acquired as a trick. Business is sometimes carried through in a quicker way than in Europe or the United States, and the term the "land of *mañana*" has often been over-applied, at least as regards business transactions.

Again, it must be recollected that the Ibero-American—with a touch perhaps of Orientalism—does not always like to give a direct "yes" or "no." In the latter case, perhaps, he does not wish to hurt his visitor's feelings, and may leave him to infer a negative from the general conversation. This should be understood, and a direct reply not sought.

On the other hand, this method of courtesy does not necessarily apply to all operations of dealing. The rudeness of the shop-hand in Latin American towns is a matter of note often; his brusqueness and incivility. It is possible that this may arise in part from the custom of haggle; that is, of not having fixed prices for articles sold, and the customer, especially women, enter and argue to a wearisome length often, in obtaining a reduction, or finger the goods to such an extent as to exasperate the whole race of counter attendants. Be it as it may, courtesy by the shopkeeper is not a marked condition here. There are, of course, exceptions.

We shall also remark a further condition. The Latin American is generally more urbane in his conduct than the Spaniard. The pure Iberian is often a very direct fellow, blunt of speech and behaviour. Often his speech, when excited, is interlarded with the most tremendous oaths.

These matters of deportment are not necessarily intricate, and they should not be overdone. Frankness and sincerity always appeal. The Spanish

American wishes to appear to be direct. He will tell you he is so. *Yo soy franco, señor*—"I am frank," he will frequently exclaim in the course of any argumentative conversation, or, *Vamos á ser practicos*—"let us be practical." It does not, of course, follow that he is always either frank or practical. Often, however, he is.

The Englishman generally finds that prejudice is in his favour in these circles. The *Ingles* has a name for fair and straightforward dealing (which Heaven grant always is and always may be deserved!). Here we have the well-known and oft-quoted aphorism of the *Palabra de Ingles*; that is, the "word of an Englishman," which is reputedly held to be as good as his bond. He is supposed to carry out, without chicanery or mental reservation, what he has undertaken to do. His goods will be up to the sample; his fulfilment as his promise. He will often find this national trait appraised here, and often with disparagement of the methods of the traders of other nationalities, and this not merely as a form of subtle flattery.

Whether this high standard is always now kept, under the pressure of increasing competition, it may be left to others to determine.

Again, the excellence of British manufacture is generally looked upon as a foregone conclusion.

Cheap goods, such as textiles, however, in the face of this competition, wherever they come from, are probably often very free from reproach, and an enormous quantity of cheap rubbish must find its way on to the backs of the poorer wearers in these lands, of British and other manufacture.

Against the British manufacturer there is always the old outstanding accusation that he does not sufficiently regard the tastes or needs of his clients overseas, but adopts a "take-it-or-leave-it attitude," and this is a point writers on the subject generally bring forward. Doubtless it has been somewhat exaggerated.

Again, another theme is that of disregard of the important matters of packing, both as to external appearances of boxes and packages which are to be exposed for sale and the packing for means of transport such as the exigencies of the road call for here.

Many writers on British trade take it upon themselves to disparage their own methods and institutions, but this has been overdone. If there are defects in British methods, they occur equally in those of the traders of other nations. However, self-disparagement is a British characteristic in many things, and may readily be discounted.

The subject of finance, credits and so forth are matters which always come up for discussion here. Long credits are often necessary, especially in the case of the smaller merchants or dealers of Latin America, and in the smaller towns, where these have not capital for quick payments and the goods have to be sold before a return is reaped. There may be bad debts often, or dishonest customers, but as a rule the purchasing store-keeper is often kept in the path of rectitude by the knowledge that dishonesty will result in cutting off his supplies sooner or later, with consequent ruination.

To return to business. It is an error to suppose that the Latin American is lacking in enterprise, for the reverse is generally the case.

Again, the folk of these lands we are here treading are exceedingly assimilative of new ideas and novelties. They like to be thought "up-to-date." New appliances and luxuries catch their fancy. Motor-cars, gramophones, cinematographs and so forth are eagerly purchased. Were the roads better, bicycles would have had an enormous vogue, and may yet have. Aeroplanes are likely to be very prominent things in the future. Anything new, fashionable or pleasurable is regarded with favour, from notepaper to flying machines.

It is, however, noteworthy that the deeper refinements of life are less considered. Thus the Latin American folk are not great readers of books or purchasers of pictures. Nor have they a great love for antiques. It is true that books published in Spanish (or Portuguese) are generally limited in range and miserably printed and bound, and it is probable that a foreign publisher who should undertake to cater to a growing literary appetite here would find in it a remunerative business. Something, of course, has been done in this way, especially in Argentina, where imports of books from Britain have increased rapidly.

As to pictures, gaudy oleographs and calendars often do duty for these. But the love of pictures for themselves seems to have diminished at the present time among all peoples, even in Anglo-Saxondom: perhaps it has fled before more material delights; perhaps it may return.

The British Governmental attitude towards trade abroad—and Latin America naturally takes an important place—somewhat halts between two opinions, as concerns official representation. Shall British representatives be mainly diplomatic, ambassadorial, or shall they also descend to that less distinguished field of commerce? Shall the atmosphere of the Minister Plenipotentiary or that of the more commercialized Consul be paramount?

England—Britain—is constantly upbraided by traders and trade-writers on account of her alleged supineness with regard to foreign trade. We are accused of not doing enough, of not having sufficiently active representatives abroad, of not attending to the wants of foreign purchasers, of not knowing their languages, of not sufficiently pressing our wares upon them, and so forth.

But when all is said that can be said upon this subject, it must be recollected that Britain has had a very prosperous day as the workshop of the world, and has greatly enriched herself in foreign markets. There seems little doubt that she is disposed to rest somewhat on her laurels now. Apart from this, there are physical causes why it is difficult for Britain to pretend to hold predominance here, as well as sociological reasons. A steady export trade should be aimed at, not a feverish attempt at perpetual predominance.

We turn now to the important matters of foreign investment and finance in these widely diversified lands of Latin America.

The statistics of finance inform us that, among the oversea enterprises of the British capitalist, more than a thousand million pounds sterling are invested in stocks, bonds and shares in undertakings in the Republics of Latin America; securities quoted upon the London Stock Exchange. There are further enterprises not so quoted. From this considerable sum a steady stream of dividends flows to Great Britain, amounting to over eighty million pounds per annum.

In these statistics we have an indication of the great activity that has taken place in the past by the British individual, or joint-stock company in this field, from Mexico to Peru or Chile, from Venezuela and Colombia to Brazil or the River Plate.

Wherever we journey in Spanish America, we shall find our countrymen engaged in some important enterprise or industry. If we ascend to the high plateau of Mexico it will be upon an English owned and operated railway, from the coast of Vera Cruz, which we have reached upon an English steamer. If we enter the rich mines here we shall see English capital extracting gold and silver, which flows to London, and other minerals too. If we survey Mexico City, we shall see that it and its lake-basin is drained by a wonderful canal and tunnel, a work which the Aztecs and the early Spaniards tried to perform but failed in, and do we cross from sea to sea over the Tehuantepec Isthmus it will be upon a railway rebuilt, with fine harbours at each approach—a competitor, in some respects, with the Panama Canal—by English engineers and money, whilst the electric lights and trams of the capital are nourished from the same source. (The tramway system, indeed, from the *centavos* of the travelling Mexican poor, pay or did pay the working costs before nine o'clock in the morning, leaving the rest of the day for the dividends.)

In South America we can scarcely take train in any of the numerous Republics without travelling over rails laid down by the genius of Albion, or without helping, in the purchase of our ticket, to contribute towards the exchequer of the British company which built or controls it. When we rise from the Spanish Main to the mountains of Venezuela or Colombia, it is upon lines made by British brains and purses; or when we go up from sea-level to the dizzy heights of the Andes of Peru or Chile, it is behind the iron horse whose trajectory or working has been rendered possible by Britain. The wonderful network of rails that traverse Brazil and Argentina, and bring forth to the seaboard the product of corn, cattle, coffee and all else, were built with gold from Lombard Street, as were the docks and harbours whence they discharge their wealth of products from the hinterland. Again, if we penetrate the dark reaches of the Amazon, England is giving gas light, electric light, water supply, dock service and much else there; and we shall have ascended that mighty stream on an English steamer. Nay, some of the rubber of these forests is extracted by the power of British gold. Banks are largely British.

England, in brief, has performed an enormous service in the New World with her money. The United States built itself up on British capital, so that every Republic in America has had cause for gratitude for the use of English gold. England is not a gold-producing country, but nevertheless a stream of gold has proceeded from her shores to nourish the most distant lands.[42]

CHAPTER XVI
TO-DAY AND TO-MORROW

In our travels throughout the very extensive and varied regions dealt with in these pages, we shall have remarked certain outstanding features of life characteristic in perhaps peculiar degree of the Latin American civilization. The marked division of the classes into which the social life of the Republics falls, the system of government, the distinctive architecture, civil and ecclesiastical, the peculiar mining industry—*sui generis*; the roads—or absence of such—and the special atmosphere surrounding travel in the wilds, the undeveloped condition of enormous areas of territory and their lack of population, the absence of manufacturing industry and predominance of rural occupations, the relations with foreigners, and the relations—or lack of such—of an inter-American nature; whilst there has always been before the observer interested in the sociological development of the world, the problems of the future here.

Despite eccentricities of character and difficulties of environment, we shall remark that Spanish American government and other institutions are, in general, laid down upon excellent lines, and in the future may be expected to develop in their own way.

As to government, the constitutions—written constitutions—of these States might be described almost as counsels of perfection. Theoretically they provide for all contingencies, and, were they followed, little would be amiss. Unfortunately the temperament of the Latin American people often is, that the individual will lay down the most excellent laws for the community, but apparently reserving for himself the right to contravene them, as far as he is concerned, if occasion so demand. Herein is the difficulty of self-government under the Iberian temperament.

The constitutions of the Republics are generally modelled upon that of the United States; but there is a slight difference between the associations of the various provinces or departments in some cases. Thus the Federal Republic Model, under which the provinces enjoy a species of home rule, has been adopted by Brazil, Mexico and Venezuela, whilst the remainder have what is termed the centralized form, the supreme head being the capital, with prefects set over the provinces.

The governing powers embody the executive, the legislative and the judicial; the president and his cabinet, national congress of two chambers, and a supreme tribunal. Ministers with portfolios are generally those of Foreign Affairs, Finance, Agriculture, Industry and Commerce,

Communications and Public Works, War and Marine, to which is frequently added a *Ministro de Fomento*, after the Spanish model, a department which concerns itself with the development of new industries and means of transport, land concessions, and so forth, the word meaning "encouragement" or "fostering."

A considerable bureaucracy naturally exists under this regimen, and there is a strong tendency among the educated folk to seek Government employ. On the whole, however, the system of government, with its ramifications, must be regarded as efficient and competent, and the machinery works smoothly. It is not necessarily thrown out of gear altogether by the sudden revolution or *golpe de estado*, which so frequently occurs, unless this be more than ordinarily severe. But the *caudillo*, the political leader or "boss" (to use an American equivalent) is often a corrupting and disturbing element.

With regard to the religious system, the regimen and machinery of the Romish Church is, too, well organized, from arch-bishop down to village *cura* or priest. But the education and character of this last often leaves a good deal to be desired.

As with government, so is it with education in the Latin American countries. The theory is excellent, and education is everywhere extolled, but in practice the proportion of literates, indeed of folk who can but read and write alone, is exceedingly small, amounting perhaps to ten or fifteen per cent. of the population, rising to fifty per cent. in the most advanced land, Argentina. Education is everywhere free and compulsory, and the Latin American youth can reach the universities with little cost.

The conditions of civic life in Spanish American lands are often pleasing in some essentials, and students of sociology and economics might well find matters of utility here. It might not be an exaggeration to say that there is more public spirit, of a kind, in a small Spanish American town than in its English or United States equivalent. More interest is taken in local government; there is more discussion in local matters. The inhabitant, if he has any grade of education and knowledge, thinks it natural to assert his opinion as a unit of his habitat, and public opinion is a strong factor. It is a good augury for the future.

Indeed, in the connection, it is to be noted that Spanish American people—even in circles where it would be supposed that such matters would be beyond their ken—think much and talk profoundly on questions of government, polity, economics and so forth. They display a wider range of intelligence than—for example—the lower middle-class English folk in such matters.

Useful and pleasing features in civic life are to be found in the general "town-planning" of the Latin American town or village. The Spaniards inaugurated the general plan of a central plaza or square, with streets radiating therefrom, and cross streets—the well-known "chequer board" style. It is quite possible to overdo this system, or to adhere too rigidly thereto. But the central plaza, with the church and municipal buildings, chief shops and so forth around it, is a convenient arrangement, whilst the institution of the *serenata* or open-air concert here, on Sunday afternoon and during week-day evenings, brings the people together and creates a pleasing atmosphere, and is, in fact, a social amenity of value. The plaza is the pulse of the locality.

It is, of course, to be recollected that the climate generally permits such amenities. Also, as the roads cease on the outskirts of the place, there is really nowhere else for the inhabitants to take exercise on foot. We should not like to sacrifice our typical English village, with its High Street and church on the hill, to this more stereotyped plan, but the amenities of the plaza might be much more widely copied. It has its nucleus in the village green, but the social atmosphere is lacking in this last.

The traveller in the cities and towns of Spanish America finds himself, often without knowing or analysing the cause, in an atmosphere quaint, restful and pleasing. He seems transplanted to an old-world or semi-mediaeval environment, as of some more ancient or remote place of European lands where the vulgarizing hand of the commercial age is as yet unknown. Looking around and above him he finds the sensation is imparted by the buildings, the façades of the streets, the churches and the general disposition architecturally of the place. It is the atmosphere and influence of the old Spanish Colonial architecture.

Notwithstanding the very considerable extent and interest of this field, few writers on Spanish America appear to have made any broad study of the subject, or at least to have set down much in the way of description of what is so noteworthy and important a feature of life in these widely-scattered communities, but it is a matter worthy of some study.

This type of architecture is, naturally, more intensively represented in those parts of the Spanish American Continent which were the principal seats of viceregal rule, such as Mexico and Peru, but the style predominates throughout the whole of Central and South America, and in the West Indian Islands, such as Cuba and Santo Domingo, which were under Spanish sway. The example set, the style was followed to a considerable extent after the time of Independence, and with some modification, subservient to modern economic, domestic or commercial requirements, is employed in modern erections. Here, however, a new note has been introduced, an unpleasing note, and the dignified and quaint "classic" of the Colonial architecture has to some extent given place to a cheaper-appearing "Gothic," which, beside the older style, often appears frivolous or tawdry, although its exponents may derive some satisfaction from their claim to be "modern" and "progressive." The façades of the streets—and the circumstance is notable especially in the larger cities—has in some cases been vulgarized by the erection of huge business premises or blocks, in which the utilitarian has triumphed over the dignified and chaste.

There is less call for comment on this last-named condition in such centres as Buenos Ayres and others, which have sprung to being in comparatively recent times, and even Rio de Janeiro; but even here, as in modern Rio de Janeiro, the old chaste style has been widely reproduced and perpetuated, side by side with the "commercial" order and the somewhat riotous stucco architecture of the plutocratic residence.

The principal features of the Colonial style of street architecture are the square-headed windows with their moulded architraves, and, more elaborately, pediments, and the prominent cornices, friezes and sills. The balcony to the upper windows, and the *rejas* or iron grilles, to the lower—the latter originally and indeed still a necessary safeguard, from various causes—are the most prominent features, together with the wide *saguan* or principal doorway, high enough for a mounted horseman to enter, giving access to the *patio* or courtyard, around which, generally open to the sky, the interior doors and windows are disposed—a type, of course, inherited from the Moors through Spain. The houses are built close against the street. There is no garden or space in front, but the *patio* is generally planted, often beautifully so, with shrubs and flowers, often with the addition of a fountain. Around the upper wall of the *patio* a gallery runs, reached by an outside staircase, giving access to the various apartments of the first floor.

In the public buildings, and in the more elaborate private mansions, such as the main residential streets of the capitals display, the window-heads are frequently arched. Much effect is gained by the method of severity in the greater part of the façade, with elaborate carving disposed where needful. The material is generally of stone in the older buildings, and in the newer—but with an effect that does not deceive—the scheme is carried out in plaster or stucco, whose appearance is sometimes too artificial. The most notable feature of the façades of those buildings which form the sides of the plazas, or public squares, are the *portales* or arcades, of arches supported on columns, a covered footpath thus being formed, with the upper stories of the buildings thereover. This type of building is, of course, common to Latin countries in Europe.

When we come to the church architecture of the Spanish American towns, we enter a somewhat different field. Enormous work has been lavished upon them. Their façades are sometimes loaded with the most ornate carvings, exciting admiration for the beauty and dexterity of their individual parts, but giving occasion for the criticism of being overdone and overburdened.

The cathedrals and churches of the larger Mexican cities are things to marvel at, in many instances. So intricate, beautiful and elaborate is the ornamentation which has been lavished upon these and other ecclesiastical structures, even in remote towns whose very name is unknown to the ordinary European traveller, that words fail to describe them, and they must be seen to be appreciated. The work was performed mainly in the time of the viceroys.

The temples of Peru are less noteworthy, but nevertheless follow out in some degree the same lavish style, as evidenced in the sacred edifices of Lima and to a less extent those of Cuzco and Arequipa. If Mexico was a "city of palaces" (as Humboldt termed it), Lima has at least claims to be considered a city of beautiful ecclesiastical structures.

Other Spanish American capitals may also point with pride to the beauty of their old public and consecrated buildings, and, indeed, Spanish culture in this respect, the fervour and piety of the Romish Church in Iberian hands, has conferred a benefit upon the New World for which it might well be grateful. Throughout thousands of miles of savage territory Spain caused to arise these oases of religious and monastic culture, appreciation of which the lapse of time, rather than diminishing, should augment.

Let us consider in some brief detail a few examples of the Colonial mural art. In Mexico there is such lavish wealth that we must be content with a few examples.

A building generally regarded by the Mexicans as perhaps one of the most chaste and pleasing of their public edifices, although not one of the oldest, is that of the former Temple of San Augustin, of which a picture is here given. It was erected in 1692, and, after the time of the Reform, when ecclesiasticism was dispossessed, it became, by mandate of President Juarez, the Biblioteca Nacional, or Public Library of the city of Mexico. The lower portion is Ionic, the upper partakes of the Churrigueresque style, which predominated in New Spain from the sixteenth century, replacing the severer architecture prior to that period.

Here, amid the two hundred thousand volumes of the library, are documents, little known and unprinted, containing valuable matter concerning the early history of America.

In contrast with the moderately severe style of the above is the façade of the principal entrance of the Sagrario, or Basilica Metropolitana, intricately sculptured portals of majestic character, a network of carved pilasters and figures, a typical work of Churriguera, which compels the admiration of the visitor. It is built of the red *tezontle* stone, compact and clear-hued, adding to its ornate beauty.

The temple abuts upon the garden of the cathedral. This splendid structure is the finest from some points of view, of its nature, in the whole of America, north or south. Its two great towers, rising for two hundred feet from the pavement, are landmarks far and wide throughout the Valley of Mexico. It is four hundred feet long and two hundred wide, in the form of a Greek cross, with two naves and three aisles and twenty-two side chapels. The vaulted roof is supported by twenty Doric columns, and its great candelabra of gold, silver and copper, altars, rare paintings and other appointments, render it a notable example of church architecture.

There are sixty massive churches in Mexico City, and as many more old convents and monasteries, or such was their original purpose before they were turned over to secular uses by the Reform. The domes—for many are domed—and towers of the ancient buildings stand out finely from the mass of the city, as beheld from the hills which surround the valley, bearing witness to the devout, the fanatic, the love of the beautiful which inspired Mexico under the viceroys. The cathedral was erected to face the great Zocalo or plaza on whose site stood the Teocalli or pyramid of the Aztec war god, a scene of bloody rites and barbarous sacrifice, stormed by Cortes and his Spaniards and razed to the ground.

The view here given of one of the side streets of the Mexican capital serves to show the type of severe street architecture before described, and affords a glimpse of the towers of the cathedral. Upon the street, face old residences of Spanish nobles or viceroys, and one side of the Palacio Nacional, formerly the residence of Cortes. The solid blocks of red *tezontle* of which they are built, so largely employed in the Viceregal period, give a sombre aspect to this broad thoroughfare, lightened somewhat by the white habit of the Indian porters on the pavement.

STREET IN MEXICO CITY. CATHEDRAL IN DISTANCE.

Vol. II. To face p. 264.

A beautiful edifice, open to the public by reason of its use as the principal hotel of the city, is the Hotel Iturbide, the former residence of that short-lived and ill-fated emperor of Mexico. Its interior patio, surrounded by colonnades, is typical of this class of dwelling, and the slender column and symmetry of its arches are such as arrest the visitors' gaze.

Yet another type of public building, remarkable in its solidity and massive beauty, is the great Edificio de Mineria, as it is now termed, being used as a school of engineers, an institution of which Mexico has been justly proud. This fine building dates from the end of the eighteenth century, when the Colonial period was expiring, and it is typical of the severe style of the period. Tolsa, the architect of this and some other Mexican buildings, took his inspiration from Rome and Greece.

The wonders of Mexican Colonial architecture are not monopolized by the capital. We may find in the remote towns examples as remarkable, whether in the great northern towns of the plateau, whether in the States of Oaxaca and Vera Cruz, places where the traveller might pass many pleasing hours, but unknown to the outside world.

A feature of the architecture, or rather decorative scheme, of Spanish American houses, which the traveller will not fail to note, is that of the use of colour on the exterior. This, however, is not employed on the well-built or stone structures, but mainly on those of the plastered adobe dwellings of the lower middle and poorer classes, although old Government palaces and public buildings often have a wash or tint over their faces. Architraves of painted blue or red, panelling in orange, generous rose-tints over the whole façade are to be seen, especially in the smaller towns and the villages.

This custom of exterior house painting is, of course, from Spain and the Moors. Whilst it may be objected to as being gaudy, nevertheless it is often pleasing and picturesque, relieving the drab aspect of the streets. The adobe wall is, naturally, plastered with some material, lime or in some cases—as at Oruro—kaolin, thus presenting a smooth surface for the colour. The colour material may be paint, or, generally, a kind of "distemper" or wash.

The effect is an unfamiliar one to the English or North American traveller, accustomed to the severe and colourless aspect of his own streets, but looking along these Spanish American thoroughfares or highways and byways of the towns—which are often the framing for a distant picture of a far-off Cordillera, blue in the distance, or a snow-capped peak, or a piece of tawny desert—the colour scheme is rather an added element in the general effect.

We find this custom largely in Mexican towns, in Central America, in Peru, Bolivia and the Cordillera generally—in brief, almost everywhere.

CHAPEL OF THE ROSARIO, MEXICO.

Vol. II. To face p. 266.

From the towns we come naturally to the roads. Of the "philosophy of the road" in Spanish America, I have spoken elsewhere.

It will be impressed upon us in our travels in the wild regions of Spanish America that, however fruitful Nature may be here, we cannot adequately enjoy these fruits until means of transport and communication are more plentiful and easier. There are thousands of miles of territory where the sound of the locomotive has never been heard, where, indeed, neither road nor bypath exists. The difficulties of railway and highway building here are often immense. The topography of the country is against it; the geological formation, the climate offer serious obstacles. Precipitous hills and unstable ground and torrential rainfall render almost impossible in places either the construction or maintenance of any form of highway.

Yet we shall doubt if the limit of human ingenuity has been reached here, and greater inventive and mechanical genius must be brought to bear on the problem, in new types of road and railway. The engineer is somewhat apathetic in this connection, whether in America or Europe.

The people of Spanish America seem unable to do much for themselves in the building of railways. No line is ever built except by British gold and foreign engineers. They could do much more themselves, especially as regards roads.

Will air-navigation help to solve the problem of transport in South America? Perhaps, to a limited extent. Aeroplane services might be of inestimable value in rendering communication possible with the sequestered towns of the Cordillera, for example. There are vast open spaces where landing would be easy, given the overcoming of atmospheric difficulties. Some investigation is beginning. In Peru some study of the possible routes among the mountains has been made. In Chile the Andes have been crossed by an airman. Flying, although possibly its "circus" attributes are most attractive, appeals to the temperament of the Spanish American. But a Peruvian airman[43] strove to be the first to cross the Alps, and gallantly perished in the attempt. Brazil also furnished its pioneer airman.[44] Hydroplanes might be of service, as they could alight on the rivers, in crossing the Amazon forests.

A glance now at the mining industry, so largely dependent upon means of transport here.

It cannot be said that gold plays a predominant part in the mining of to-day in the Latin American countries. More important is the winning of the baser metals.

It is, in fact, somewhat remarkable that a land, fabled earlier for its plenitude of gold, should in modern times, yield so relatively small an output. The value of the whole gold production of the Latin American countries scarcely reaches the annual amount of £8,000,000, which shrinks into insignificance beside the £50,000,000 of a single group of mines in another continent, the South African Rand. Of this, Mexico produces three-quarters, leaving the vast continent of South America with the small sum, as contribution to the world's stock of the yellow metal, of some two million pounds' sterling only.

We may inquire as to the reason of this paucity, and the reply, in the first instance undoubtedly is that, although Nature has placed gold in the rocks and soils of Central and South America in almost every quarter, the metal is in a form that does not always lend itself to the winning in large bulk. The mines are rich, but often small and scattered. There have not here been discovered the enormous bodies of ore which, although of low grade, as in South Africa, by their very extent and compactness, render mining economically and physically a more profitable undertaking. Further, it may be said that, in more recent times, mining enterprise and the attention of capital needful for such has not been drawn so strongly to the possibilities of gold-mining in the Latin American countries, and, lastly, political unrest and revolution in these States has in some cases rendered it precarious.

This last condition need not be exaggerated. It may be said that the Governments of the Latin American Republics are, in the main, generous in their treatment of foreign mining enterprise in their territories, and that sporadic revolution does not necessarily seriously affect the working of the mines, though at times it may cause temporary inconvenience and possible loss. The foreign shareholders of the few considerable gold mines of South America, and even of Mexico, have in general reaped excellent returns on their investments. Conditions in Mexico, however, of late have been intolerable in some cases, with confiscation and even murder attending them.

We have remarked the need of a greater population in the Latin American States, and the Governments of these in most cases strive to obtain settlers and workers from Europe, offering often what appear to be attractive conditions for immigrants. In Argentina the modern life of the Republic has in large part been built upon this element, largely of Italians, and the national character stands somewhat apart from the other States from this reason. Brazil has also absorbed many immigrants of the Latin race from the Old World, and the Germans here, and in Chile, have formed important communities.

But much remains to be done in this respect. It is seen that a good deal of the immigrant population in Argentina and Brazil remains as a floating or unsettled element. Much of it does not go out upon the land, but congregates in poverty in the cities—a defect of all immigrant systems, even in the British Dominions. In Argentina and Brazil immigrants often cannot obtain land, although the Governments are seeking to modify the conditions of vast estate holding and the rural proletariat.

It may be that the stream of emigrating humanity from Europe will not flow so freely in the future, in view of altering conditions on the older continent. Of late, too, the larger South American States are inclining towards the restriction of immigration.

The opportunities for settlement, for taking up land and establishing industry and reaping reward and profit in Spanish America are, or rather might be, attractive. They might be, in some respects, more attractive than those offered by Britain's colonies, for reasons which I will give.

Why are these opportunities not taken? Here are enormous areas of territory full of natural resources, with, in some cases, a mere handful of folk to the square mile. Here are natural pastures for cattle, lands which will produce fruits and foods of every kind—figs, grapes and oranges, cotton, coffee, cocoa, corn and wine and olives. Not a variety of fruit, not a cereal, not a single article of need for the comfort and use of the settler is there that could not be produced. Here are minerals of every kind known to commerce—gold, silver, copper, lead and iron, and all the non-metallic minerals—to be had for the working.

But above all, there are innumerable small centres of population, of quiet and docile folk, hungering for the presence of intelligent and enterprising settlers who would look kindly upon them, who would foster their local life, increase the productivity of the neighbourhood, take part in their civic and economic advancement. Nowhere in the world is there such desire for these things, nowhere is there such opportunity for the settler for benefiting both himself and the folk around him as is to be found in the innumerable little villages and towns of Spanish America hidden away in Cordillera, plain, valley and woodland. There are literally myriads of such localities scattered over the face of the Latin American world, and I could give many instances from personal experience.

The well-meaning foreigner in such places, with some small capital, becomes one of the most esteemed and predominant personages of the locality. He could acquire and profit by flocks, herds, plantations, mines. There is plenty of labour, among the Indian and other folk, to be obtained—labour, that is, in small local undertakings, not for over-greedy or absorbent joint-stock operations—under the relation of master and servant. Here is an opportunity, then, for those good English and other folk who complain so hardly of heavy taxation and other burdens of life! Any degree of climate may be chosen, from heat to cold, including the "region of perpetual spring," of which we have spoken elsewhere.

It is not intended here to advocate settlement in Spanish America as against the British colonies. The field is scarcely suitable for the settler who has to depend upon his own labour, without capital. He could not possibly compete with the native. The difference is, that here are innumerable old-established centres of population, centres of civic life, and not, as in Canada or Australia, vast areas of unsettled territory where the lonely colonist is remote from social amenities. Moreover, with every desire to people the British Empire with settlers from Britain, it is also to be recollected that British settlers in Spanish America increase the prestige—and incidentally the trade—of Britain in those lands—matters which should be encouraged. In Mexico, in better times, there was something about the atmosphere and environment that very strongly attracted the American settler, and large numbers of people from the United States established themselves in the country—conditions which unfortunately do not now exist.

In this connection we might ask ourselves a serious question as regards Mexico. Have we, the more advanced nations of the world, who mainly by reason of climate and geography have been blessed with a different temperament, made any particular effort to help that country, or tried to influence its people? We have invested our money there, with the hope of dividends. We have maintained our more or less starchy diplomatic representatives. We have issued Foreign Office Reports abounding in figures and pointing out the ways of trade and the resources of the land. But have we tried to influence the country to a better life?

It may be replied that we could not readily do so, that one country cannot mix itself up in the affairs of another. But that is not a sufficient answer. We have been content to take profits from railways and mines, but among the rude and picturesque hordes of Mexican miners, an impressionable and really industrious folk, there might have been some good element at work maintained by a little of the gold we won from them. Is the mine manager or the book-keeper, busied necessarily on the technical details of his post, the only agent we might have kept there?

The same reflection may be made as regards the other Latin American States, with a word of warning to directors and shareholders. The native miners are a hardy and often turbulent race. If they were not hardy they would not be miners, and if they were not headstrong they would not be likely to undertake the onerous and dangerous livelihood of the mines. These folk are, as regards "labour" ideas, mostly ignorant and unorganized at present. Directly they learn their power, and directly some greater amount of education filters in among them—accompanied, as is ever the case, by socialistic or even anarchic ideas—they will begin to demand their "rights." (The nitrate-workers in Chile, for example). Such ideas might spread very rapidly among these impressionable folk, and they would be likely to stop at nothing once the spark of disorder were kindled, even to Bolshevism of the brown race. Let us be wise in time and study the methods, before too late, by which their lot may be improved and their intelligence better directed under a wider spirit of economic instruction and justice. We may not like to face these eventualities, but that will not influence the march of events.

The same holds good with every form of foreign investment in Latin America—railways, plantations and all else. So I would venture to say, if we expect always to draw dividends from our investments in Spanish America, let us wisely have more regard to the social and economic status of the worker. How, practically, that is to be done is a question of our own intelligence. Perhaps some advisory body might be instituted in London, financed by the large British interests in Latin America, such as would devote itself to the study of the conditions of life surrounding the workers in those lands, or at least as regards their own employees. I offer this suggestion on behalf of the poorer folk of these lands. They generally look to the "Ingles" as a person of influence—one, moreover, whose pockets are always, they imagine, lined with silver! In their way these folk believe that *noblesse oblige* (in their own term for that concept) is a universal axiom of the Englishman, and there is something almost pathetic in this faith in a foreigner. Let us beware that by negligence or greed we do not forfeit this esteem. I offer the suggestion also as a contributory safeguard to British investment here.

Apart from the attitude of the individual worker in these communities in relation to foreign capital, we shall be well advised to keep in touch with the attitude not only of the workers as a whole but of the Governments which control national affairs. Of late there have been certain indications that a policy of antagonism towards foreign capital and enterprises is growing up. It has been very marked in Mexico, but in Argentina, a much more advanced community, and in the Brazilian States it is at times disquieting. It is not so much antagonism, however, as a feeling of dissatisfaction that the earnings from national or public works should go to foreign shareholders. The Argentine railways of late years have felt a good deal this disturbing element; as also the burden of numerous strikes. British capital was the pioneer in building railways in the republic, and has conferred enormous benefit upon it. More than 15,000 miles of line are owned by British companies, or three times as much as the remaining mileage, which is French and national mainly. Whilst these railways are, it is generally conceded, worked and controlled as economically and efficiently as ever, it cannot be said that they are undertakings so profitable as should cause envious eyes to be cast upon them. For the past few years the average net return of these British-owned railways in Argentina has not exceeded the modest amount of three and a half per cent. This is a low return, especially for Argentina, where two or three times the yield is obtained on ordinary safe mortgages on houses and land. The British-owned banks in South America may yield twenty per cent. profit. Yet voices arise in the land, asking why the transport of the country should be conducted for the interests of foreign shareholders, and begin to demand a larger share. A cry of this kind soon becomes general, and when a government has come into power on the strength of popular promises—and to obtain votes and power this condition arises now in South America, as in all other lands—it has to attempt to carry out its promises, and the line of least resistance here is sometimes the foreign corporation. There is one simple remedy which discontented governments and folk here could apply—in purchasing for themselves the shares of the railway companies in the open market, but it does not appear that this legitimate operation is much indulged in.

With regard to the native labour, it is to be recollected that there are few (or no) laws to safeguard it from exploitation by the employer. It is only just beginning to learn how to combine in its own interest. As I have shown in these pages, it is in many instances and throughout the whole region often over-exploited. The upper-class employer, the Spanish American, does not lack kindliness and charity, but it is contrary to his custom and outlook to think much of the labourer. The Spaniard and the Portuguese have been oppressive in this connexion throughout history.

Strikes in Argentina and Uruguay have of late become very bitter in character, and bloodshed generally occurs. Trains have been derailed and passengers and drivers fired upon. It is to be recollected that labour is not necessarily all of the native stock, but is supplemented by the flow from turbulent Spanish and Italian sources. The poor Iberian or Calabrian comes over with a sense of wrong against society, which in his own lands he often has good reason to nourish, and which he cannot throw aside on this new soil as readily as he may the picturesque native costume of his fatherland. In this respect we might indeed say—*Coelum non animum mutant qui trans mare currunt*. The great estuary of the River Plate receives in its haven many a discontented emigrant, many an agitator from the Latin lands of Europe, whose social defects, national and individual, by a curious combination of circumstance, many an English home—holder of shares in Argentine and Brazilian railways—is, in a sense, called upon to expiate!

There can be little doubt, moreover, that the reins of power in certain South American States tend to fall more and more into the hands of politicians of a very democratic type—not to say socialistic—and as the education of the "proletariat" increases this element is likely to increase. The Cabinet formed of "doctors," of the upper and select strata of society, men of distinguished type—but often out of touch and indeed sympathy with the masses of their poorer countrymen—and of military men, also of the upper strata, is likely to be more and more diluted with the ruder element who bears, sincerely or for political purposes, the social wrongs of his constituents as his creed. In brief, we may expect to see in Latin America a wave of that unrest which now has submerged Russia, perhaps Germany, and which in some degree threatens every land. Let us hope that, before it is too late, the channels of human intelligence will flow with a true spirit of humanity and the milk of human kindness and order. But the general world-outlook is not encouraging, and no doubt there is yet to be bitter experience in these lands of Cancer and Capricorn, of Central and South America, in the development of their social affairs.

The relations of foreigners with the Latin American people opens a wide field of discussion, upon which we may lightly touch.

The social culture of these communities in the past has been most greatly influenced by French ideas, and France is still the ideal nation. It may be that France, by reason of her apostasy and her expulsion of the religious orders from her shores in recent time, has lost prestige however.

The relations of the Americans of the United States with the people of Latin America present a number of interesting conditions and problems. The two types of people and their civilizations differ from each other in every respect, yet, neighbours on the same continent and twin-continent, they are and in the future will be more and more thrown into contact with each other. The situation is such as that which would arise if England and Spain or England and France found themselves with a common frontier, that of only a small river, or the imaginary one of a parallel of latitude between them. This is exemplified on the Mexico-United States border, where the two races, the Spanish American and the Anglo-Saxon American—if that term may be correctly applied to the people of the United States—come into contact but do not assimilate.

The first problem is one of nomenclature. The people of the United States have arrogated to themselves the name of "Americans," although, of course, this belongs equally to all inhabitants of the New World. The Latin Americans do not necessarily agree with the pretension, and have among themselves applied the term *Norteamericanos* to their northern neighbours—that is, "North Americans." This alternates with the term *Yanquis*, the hispanicized form of the soubriquet "Yankee," of doubtful origin; not, however, necessarily used in a derogatory fashion, but familiarly. The word *gringo* is also a common term applied to the Americans; not, however, to them alone, but to any foreigner not of Latin race. The origin of this term is obscure, and it cannot be said to be a flattering designation. The word is often meant, however, as describing a person whose hair and eyes are not dark, contrasting thus with the general type of the Latin American. Blue eyes and blonde hair are essentially *gringo*.

The Americans of the United States, as has often been pointed out, are a people without a distinctive or appropriate race name. The Canadian, the Mexican, the Brazilian, the Peruvian and all other units of America have their own designation. So far no term for the American has developed, and convenience warrants the usage of that they have adopted, which is as if a single nation of Europe were to take to itself the name European. To the American aborigine, whether in the Northern or Southern continent, ethnologists have applied the term *Amerind*, a contraction of "American Indian," and the word seems to have been adopted, at least as a technical term. (No one, however, has applied the name "Amersaxon" to the people of the United States, although it would be equally correct.)

The relation between the two races, or rather the common possession of the New World by them, has given rise to that peculiar and well-known policy or system known as the Monroe Doctrine. Washington recommended the policy that the United States should refrain from entangling itself in the politics of Europe. The converse, that Europe should be prevented from meddling in American affairs, grew as the importance of the United States increased, and was enunciated—after a hint from Canning—by President Monroe, in a message to Congress in 1823, at the time of the "Holy Alliance" of European Powers, which it was feared would attempt to restore the dominion of Spain to the Spanish American colonies, which had asserted their independence. "We should consider any attempt on their part (the European Powers) to extend their system to any portion of this hemisphere as dangerous to our peace and safety. With the existing colonies of any European Power we have not interfered and shall not interfere. But with the Governments who have declared their independence we could not view any interposition for the purpose of oppressing them or controlling their destiny by any European Power in any other light than as the manifestation of an unfriendly disposition towards the United States." So ran the decree.

The Latin American States, whilst probably not ungrateful for the Doctrine in general, resent any assertion of hegemony upon the part of the United States. They do not regard themselves as in any way inferior thereto, except as concerns the material development of the more mechanical arts of civilization. Their own social culture, the traditions of the *caballero*, or gentleman, they consider as superior, and if truth must be told, it is so in some respects. The people of the United States—and Canada—have preferred the less-polished and more practical outlook and social port; the Spanish American the more reserved and ceremonious. Indeed, the southern folk often regard the northerner as uncultured. There is no doubt that the two races have a good deal to learn from each other, the southerner in the practical things of life, the northerner in social amenities, and each could well absorb some of the virtues of the other.

Until very recent times there was a disposition on the part of the Spanish American people to imagine the northerner as disposed to overrun them, and there was an element in the United States which undoubtedly had such purpose before it. But probably this is past, and the idea that the Monroe Doctrine of "America for the Americans" meant in reality "America for the North Americans," may die out. The judicious and generous attitude of the United States in Cuba after the war between the United States and Spain has been put against the methods employed, for example, in the case of Panama and the Canal. Mexico, however, remains a difficult question, upon whose future relations with her neighbour it would be impossible to dogmatize. The United States at the present time are in the heyday of their commercial life, and would appear to be resolved to conquer the Latin American countries commercially. This may or may not lead to strife in the future. We shall not forget that the Great War was, in large degree, the outcome of the modern phase of commercial jealousy, and what developments the future holds we cannot foresee.

We ought not to close our survey of the Latin American nations without at least briefly recording their attitude in the Great War, in the question of right against might, of civilization against German savagery. Far out of the beaten track of European (and North American) affairs as are these growing nations, their history in this connexion might readily be forgotten, and its importance overlooked.

It was not unnatural perhaps that the Latin American Republics should have been tardy in entering into the war, in view of the attitude of the senior Republic of the Western Hemisphere—the United States—which hung so long in the balance. It did not at all follow that they would imitate that country. In some respects they might do so; in others they did not necessarily regard their cousin of the north with entire confidence. However, they were greatly influenced thereby.

The earlier attitude of the United States towards the war must ever remain a source of wonder to the historian, accompanied by regret. It was largely, if not principally, the result of the attitude of their President, Dr. Woodrow Wilson. It will be recollected that the United States did not enter the war against the German barbarians until April, 1917—that is, over two and a half years after the outbreak of the war. That was the period necessary for the Republic to overcome its own suspicion of Europe, and especially England; to overcome its own self-interest, to awaken to the truth; and this notwithstanding all the horrors that had been visited upon Belgium. Long after these dreadful occurrences had sunk into the mind of the Allies, who, originally unprepared for war, were fighting for their life in support of humanity against the huge organized army which Germany had for decades been building up to carry out her ambitions, the American President could send out his extraordinary Note to all the belligerents (December, 1916) stating that in his view "the objects on both sides appeared to be the same." In plain words, the respective merits of the combatants were as good or bad as each other! In this view, however, to the credit of the United States, it should be said that a large body of Americans had a much clearer moral perception of the issues at stake than their leader, and among them was the vigorous ex-President, Mr. Roosevelt. But it required a direct blow in the face for the United States before the President could shake off his pacifist attitude, and actual injury to American property and life; and this incentive was furnished by the German submarine activity and the sinking of American ships. The United States' interposition in the war had not been asked for by England and the Allies at first, but it had become evident long before that the Republic should have ranged itself on the side of law, order, and humanity; and America lost an opportunity, which may never recur, of asserting her moral influence in the world—a loss which, it may be said, is hers as much as that of Europe. The American interposition was of great value when it did come, but the bulk of the work had been done. America was almost too late to save her prestige and to take efficient part in this great adventure. When the Americans did enter they displayed great energy and valour, and it must also be recollected that the part the United States had played in the supply of munitions of war, foodstuffs, credit and so forth had been of the utmost value, and there was more in this than a mere business transaction.

The Latin American States did not necessarily hasten to follow President Wilson's implied suggestion of February, 1917, on severing diplomatic relations with Germany, that the remaining neutral States should follow suit, which no doubt was largely aimed at the southern republics. There were various reasons against it. Many of these thought their own interests would best be served by remaining neutral; some were afraid of Germany—it was not unnatural. Some were angered with France, for reasons later discussed; some were—at least clerically—pro-German. On the whole, however, it must be recorded that Latin American sympathy as a whole was, and had been from the beginning, on the side of the Allies. It would indeed have augured ill for their moral perception if the reverse had been the case, and would have seriously injured them in the eyes of historians.

Of these twenty independent Latin American States, eight actually entered the war, on the side of the Allies and the United States. They were (in alphabetical order) Brazil, Costa Rica, Cuba, Guatemala, Haiti, Honduras, Nicaragua and Panama. Five broke off relations with Germany but did not declare war. They were Bolivia, Ecuador, Peru, San Domingo (the Dominican Republic) and Uruguay. Peru and Uruguay were practically belligerents, by their various acts against Germany, but Germany did not appear so to regard them. However, both these republics were invited to the Peace Conference, and signed the Peace Treaty. Seven republics remained neutral. They were Argentina, Chile, Colombia, Mexico, Paraguay, Salvador and Venezuela.

Putting the area of Latin America at nine million square miles and the population at ninety millions (of both these items various estimates are given), it may be said that six million square miles and fifty million people were at least non-neutral.

However, such figures must be taken for what they were worth. Only Brazil and Cuba took any active part. Argentina and Chile, the two most important and powerful States after Brazil, carefully preserved their neutral attitude. (It will be recollected that the group of the three greatest Powers of Latin America, which have been termed the "A B C" Powers, are Argentina, Brazil and Chile.) Mexico, the second largest State of Latin America in point of population, was also neutral, and at one time appeared to be strongly pro-German—an attitude which was partly instrumental in influencing the United States to take up arms.

It must always be recollected, again, that the official attitude of these States—as in the case of the United States also, before it took part—did not necessarily represent that of the majority of the intelligent classes.

The actual entry of Brazil did not come until October, 1917; that of Cuba came simultaneously with that of the United States. Peru broke off relations with Germany in October; Ecuador in December; Bolivia in February (with the United States); Uruguay in October; Panama at the same period; Guatemala in April; Honduras and Nicaragua in May; Costa Rica in September; Haiti and San Domingo in July.

We may cast a glance at the various influences at work in the respective attitudes of these States towards the war.

Some of the States regarded with alarm the possibilities of a German victory as such would concern themselves. They had not forgotten that their independence was largely a result of the European outburst that followed the French Revolution, nor yet the designs of Napoleon on the Spanish American colonies and Brazil, which England had helped to thwart, and those of Spain and the Holy Alliance after Independence, which, again, England and the United States had frustrated. They knew Germany but for the Monroe Doctrine—an Anglo-American creation—would long ago have striven to help herself to South American territory. On the other hand, German propaganda had been especially active and sinister among them during the war—business men and professors—and the Germans had strong influence there. Also Spanish and other clerical influences were at work among them, often representing France as the great atheist nation, due to her anti-Church legislation and apostasy, and—for example in Chile—it was even said that Germany was the chosen instrument of heaven to punish France on this account. Further, there was always the smouldering distrust of the "Colossus of the North," the *Norteamericanos* of the United States, which it was often thought desired to exercise an undue hegemony over Latin America. Colombia retained an animus against the United States as a result of the Panama affair.

The most active spirit in Brazil on the side of the right was the eminent Brazilian statesman, Ruy Barbosa, and it was soon seen where the sympathies of Brazil lay. Submarine outrages on her merchant marine and other motives brought forth pronouncements against the German assassins, and the seizure of the large German vessels in Brazilian ports followed, and both public and official opinion led to the rupture. The Brazilian Navy co-operated with that of the Allies, and Brazil even sent forces to the Western front, and the republic assisted with supplies. As for Argentina, the war brought her enormous prosperity as a neutral, but here the neutrality was far more official than popular, and was largely motivated by the President. An episode in Argentina was in the famous *Spurlos Versenkt* Notes of the unspeakable Luxburg, the German Chargé d'Affaires in the republic, of May and July, 1917. "As regards Argentine steamers," he wrote to his Government—through the medium of the Swedish Minister at Buenos Ayres, be it noted!—"I recommend either compelling them to turn back, letting them through, *or sinking them without trace*." This devilishly cynical pronouncement goes down to history with that of the infamous German "scrap of paper" argument. Argentine neutral citizens were to be murdered in cold blood for German ends! The Minister received his passports, the German club in Buenos Ayres was burnt by the mob, and there was a popular demand for a break with Germany; and the Senate passed resolutions. But it ended in nothing. It has been said that President Irrigoyen's extraordinary attitude in opposing the popular mind was due to pro-German feeling—which, however, was denied; to his aversion from merely following in the wake of the United States; and from a desire to preserve Argentina from war in order that his deep-seated plans of social and economic reform might not be disturbed. Be it as it may, Argentina lost her chance.

With regard to Chile, neutrality also was profitable, in the enormous demand for her nitrates. German influence was very strong in the country, both in matters military and educational; and the clerical attribute—the Church is powerful in Chile—was also a factor, as before remarked. But a large element viewed Germany with detestation, and the republic "reserved its right to act in the event of hostility against her vessels." However, Chile also lost her opportunity.

It is to be noted that it was the submarine policy of Germany in the direct attack upon vessels which was the determining factor in all these principal republics, from the United States downward.

The attitude of Uruguay was always pro-Ally. The Government of that country issued a noteworthy decree in defining its position: that "no American country, which, in defence of its own rights, should find itself in a state of war with nations of other continents will be treated as a belligerent." It may be said in general terms that the attitude of all these States proclaimed the principle of "American solidarity," or Pan-Americanism.

The considerable element of British whose homes or occupations are in Latin America followed the varying fortunes of the war with eagerness, for the name and fame of England is dear to these exiled sons. Their hearts were broken with the Tarapacá disaster to the British squadron, but resuscitated by the great victory of the Falkland Isles. It must not be forgotten that they, in considerable number, left their homes and occupations and came to England as volunteers early in the war. They were not grouped together as a separate force, being of so scattered an origin. But the King approved a special badge for them, and England should be grateful for their noble effort—we trust she was and is!

The effect of the war upon the Latin American States—whilst it cut off supplies at first of European manufactured goods and disorganized exchange and currency—was to cause an enormous demand for their raw materials, with corresponding increase of wealth. Even the first-named condition was a benefit in disguise, causing a development of home manufacture.

German trade in South America, for the time being, was ruined—a severe blow—a result of the British blockade. British and French trade of course suffered temporarily. The trade of the United States, on the other hand, increased: American goods replaced European, and it seemed at one time that the change might be permanent; but it was found that their goods were inferior, or at any rate less acceptable, than those of the older exporters. However, new horizons—trade, banking and so forth—opened in Latin America for the United States.

It cannot be said that the two American peoples know very much of each other. The aloofness is partly from geographical, partly from racial causes. Enormous distances separate their respective principal centres of life. New York and the city of Mexico, for example, are several thousand miles apart, although linked by more than one railway system. Huge deserts intervene, those dreadful wildernesses of Northern Mexico, on whose existence, indeed, an early president of Mexico, who distrusted the northern neighbour, was wont to congratulate his country, summing up the sentiment in his aphorism of "Between weakness and strength—the Desert!" As for communication by sea, it may be recollected that Europe is more accessible to, for example, Brazil and Argentina, than is New York. On the Pacific side of the continent the greater part of a hemisphere intervenes between the large centres of population of North and South America. From San Francisco, or other great seaports, to Callao and Valparaiso the steamer voyage occupies far more time than is necessary to cross the Atlantic. The people of Peru and Chile or Ecuador, and the people of California or Oregon are little more than names to each other, inhabitants of another world. Great stretches of undeveloped territory intervene, and through communication by rail has not yet been established, as the Pan-American Railway remains still on the lap of the future.

Among those nations which in the future may be reckoned upon as likely to display a desire for closer relations with Spanish America are the Chinese and the Japanese. The Mongolians seem to have—as before remarked—some affinity with the American Indian race, possibly by reason of some very ancient kinship or common ancestry, for it is held by ethnologists that America may have been very early peopled by Mongolians. In Peru, for example, the Chinaman readily establishes himself in business in the smaller villages (and often surrounds himself with several wives or female companions from among the Indian women). The Japanese have long cast eyes upon the upper reaches of the Amazon basin, or Montaña, of Peru and Brazil, for purposes of settlement and industry, and of late a company from Nippon has acquired a large tract of land there, with such an object. These folk are not unwelcome, or not so far, by the South Americans, who are desirous of seeing these vast and sparsely inhabited regions brought to life.

This possibility of a modern Mongolian "invasion" into the heart of South America is one which may take on greater importance in the future.

In general terms, however, it must be recollected that the Pacific Ocean is vast and wide. There is, nevertheless, a school of thought arising of late which affects to believe that the Pacific Ocean is destined to become the centre of the world's commercial activity. As this centre changed, they say, from the Mediterranean to the Atlantic, so will it change from the Atlantic to the Pacific. They regard the "basin" of the Pacific as a sort of entity, and look for enormous developments in this respect, of fleets bearing travellers and merchandise, of great interchange of products and so forth.

Whilst this view may be well-founded, I venture to think that certain natural factors have not been sufficiently taken into account. There is, first, the condition of enormous width from the Asiatic to the American shore; second, it is not sufficiently understood that this American shore, whether in North or South America, is in the nature of a narrow strip of land greatly cut off from the interior of the continents by vast mountain ranges and deserts. In North America the Sierra Nevadas and the Great American Desert have to be crossed between California and the eastern and central part of the United States, and the Rocky Mountains in Oregon and British Columbia, whilst in Mexico the Western Sierra Madre offers a similar obstacle. In South America, as we have seen, the Andes is a perfect mountain wall, cutting off the interior absolutely from the narrow and comparatively infertile Pacific littoral. The natural outlet of the vast area of South America is to the east; it falls to the Atlantic, not to the Pacific. Where, then, are the people and the products that would give rise to so great a movement upon the Pacific Ocean?

Lastly, I am inclined to doubt (although I may be in error) whether the future of the world is to show a vast increase in overseas trade and trafficking such as would change its centre of gravity in this respect. There are factors against such—as have been discussed in the chapter dealing with trade; factors of the natural development of self-supply, as against import of commodities, factors of the huge and increasing cost of transport, scarcity of fuel and so forth. Moreover, what does Asia want from America, or America from Asia? Both continents produce the things of the temperate and the tropic zones; both are capable of manufacturing the finished goods which they require.

Taking all these matters into consideration, it may be doubted if the Pacific Ocean is to attain to the great importance which some have imagined for it, although doubtless its traffic will increase.

A glance now towards the future of these great lands beneath the Southern American sun, and our task will be done. What is to be their future; what part are they to play in the great scene-shifting of the developing world?

First we shall have remarked that the Latin American people are material in the making. They are not a worn-out race; they are, rather, unformed, plastic, with their life before them. Second, they inhabit perhaps the richest portion of the surface of the globe, which, so far from being exhausted, has not been heavily drawn upon in some respects. It is true that coal, that adjunct of the civilization of the industrial age, is not plentiful (except in certain districts). But the future may not be so largely dependent upon this mineral. Possibly, moreover, Nature had a purpose in the absence of coal, ordaining that at least one of the world's continents should not undergo the terrors of the factory age!

Let us turn now to certain more general conditions.

The growth of the Latin American republics might seem to offer a future for the growth and even regeneration (and some writers have said the predominance again) of the Latin races in the world generally. Here, at least, is an enormous territory, some of the richest and most fertile on the globe, at present but thinly inhabited. By the close of the present century it might be that South America would contain 250 million people. A century ago there were but 15 millions. Of course the enormous growth of the population in Europe and the United States has been a result of the machine, or industrial age—by no means an unmixed good. This has depended upon the resources of coal, iron and so forth in their soils, and statistics and forecasts show that these resources, under the present system of depletion and waste, especially in England and the United States, will tend to exhaustion in a few generations. Whether that will lead to a corresponding decline in population remains to be seen, but in this and other respects it may be said that coming events cast their shadows before. Probably the greatest reproach that can be placed upon Anglo-Saxon life to-day is that we are drawing heavily upon the exhaustible resources of the earth without establishing the basis of a permanent or adequate civilization.

It should be urged that the time has come when we should take a more comprehensive, judicious and constructive outlook upon the world—its natural resources and its folk. We are inclined to think that Nature's resources, because partly unexplored here and there, are "exhaustless." The Spanish American people are fond of speaking of their *inagotable riqueza natural*—their "inexhaustible natural resources"; but these are not inexhaustible, as I have elsewhere remarked. We need a survey, a stocktaking, of the earth's resources; we need to conserve, to economize them. It is a remarkable fact, however, that the latest pronouncement of the League of Nations contains no idea or suggestion of a fundamental policy of retrenchment, conservation, development of these potentialities. The pronouncement, which seems to be largely an echo of President Wilson's original "Fourteen Points"—which doubtless had among them certain merits at the time of their enunciation—does not get beyond advocating "increased production," the "entire removal of all economic barriers," in this respect. In brief, it is the old dreary doctrine, largely, of creating and selling, of forcing goods on communities and folk who do not necessarily need them, without any scientific outlook upon the native potentialities and requirements, or the world's natural divisions—a dreadful "internationalism" which we hoped was declining. The League of Nations, as regards its economic knowledge and spirit, is a magnificent opportunity wasted, or will be so unless it develops into something far more fundamentally intelligent. This matter of outlook by so important a body is of vital importance to the Latin American States, as to all others. The exploitation of the great remaining natural resources of these countries—as is the case with many others—cannot be successfully done under the present relations of labour and capital. Capital must have its fair reward, labour must be fairly paid; but the two things at present clash, and we shall have to find the way out before the enormous, but not fruitless, wilderness of South America and Mexico can yield up what they contain. The cream of the earth's resources has been skimmed everywhere; the remainder calls for much more scientific consideration.

Indeed, it is impossible to forecast what the future of the world—which has been shaken to its foundations by recent events—is to be. Civilization may advance or it might recede, or hang fire for centuries. That depends upon the efforts and the conscience of mankind. It may be that a quieter, less strenuous life awaits it, with less of material activity and more of moral and intellectual growth. In fact, some of us who have studied the world in its economic and political aspects, will doubt if the present type of civilization has not reached its apogee and is to enter on some other phase, a phase which we believe and hope is to be of the nature indicated.

If that be so, there is no reason why the Latin American States should not acquire growing importance. The character of their more thoughtful and educated classes is towards such a life, whilst the resources of Nature they command could afford them everything needful for their existence. The Spanish American lands have been dowered with every variety of climate and product, and by going up or down their valleys their folk can gather every known food-product or thing of the animal, vegetable and mineral world.

As to their character for national turbulence, it has been shown in these pages that such disturbing influences are but the activities of a relatively small class. Their ideals are high, their aim is towards a high civilization. Some of the nations of the Old World that considered themselves foremost in civilization—such as Germany and Austria—have shown by their actions that they can fall lower in barbarity than any of the most backward nations. Moreover, all nations are restless, all their cultures are in the melting-pot, all are at fault. There must be regeneration and reconstruction everywhere.

The future of the world will be in the exercise of true spiritual factors, interwoven with or influencing what I have, elsewhere, ventured to term ethical-economic constructive principles.[45] From a wise consideration of these, there must emerge a "science of corporate life," or science of humanity, which will learn to build up the true "economic structure" of society, in conjunction with its intellectual and spiritual activities—a constructive human geography, which will aim at the true and final reaction of mankind from its environment. Elemental forces are at work, for good or ill, at the present time, and elemental forces must be met by fundamental principles. One nation to-day is almost as far from such a philosophy as another, although to-morrow might see the turning of a page which should disclose its beginnings. In this evolving book of life the Latin American Republics have their opportunity, as far as the possible exercise of principle goes, with all other nations.

The problem for these nations is to bring on their own culture, avoiding, if possible, the errors of Europe and the United States: that is, avoiding the factors of industrial unrest and economic waste that have accompanied progress. They could profit by example and experience gained by these other lands: to bring on the education and economic uplifting of the backward masses of their people, not by crowding them into factories or refusing them a living wage, not by drawing so heavily on their fruitful soils as to begin to exhaust these, but by methods more in accordance with those principles which alone can ensure permanence and nobility.

We have seen that the Latin American nations have been dowered by Providence with everything that could make a people prosperous and contented, if wisely disposed. In some respects their circumstances are superior to those of Europe and Asia. They have no over-powerful or rapacious neighbours, no chasms of race or religion to divide them, no insensate trade rivalries—things such as in the Old World have wrought such havoc with mankind. To the traveller who has sojourned in these lands it will always remain a matter of interest to see how their lives develop, what fortune or vicissitudes befall them. Under any circumstances, they offer a field of abiding interest—scenic, natural, antiquarian—and their folk are likely ever to retain the traits which attract us. Commerce and business will doubtless grow and expand between them and the Old World, or their neighbours of the United States, with corresponding benefits, but there are many features of the region which fortunately will never fall under the domain of business. One thing, again, which humanity needs is more intercourse, and Latin America is too remote from us. Books are useful, but there should be a greater interflow of people. Unfortunately, it is a feature of life now that travel becomes more rather than less expensive, and we do not know what the future may hold for or against the traveller in this connexion.

This circumstance, also, is one of those which await the more logical outlook and constructive ability of mankind, concerning the things by which we live and move and have our being.

Such, then, is the romance, reality and future of these interesting lands of the Spanish American world, as far as it has been possible to depict them in these pages.

FOOTNOTES:

[1] *Venezuela*, Dalton, South American Series.

[2] *Colombia*, Eder, South American Series.

[3] *Colombia*, op. cit.

[4] Readers of Kingsley's grand *Westward Ho!* will remember the description of La Guayra and the coast here too.

[5] The emissary was instructed to suggest the interesting trade policy of a "goods for goods" exchange: a policy which in Latin America and elsewhere might have an important future.

[6] This natural canal has been well described in *The Flowing Road*, by Caspar Whitney.

[7] *Venezuela*, op. cit.

[8] Cf. *Colombia*, op. cit. Also *Venezuela*.

[9] *Venezuela*, op. cit.

[10] *Colombia*, op. cit.

[11] *Venezuela*, op. cit.

[12] *Venezuela*, op. cit.

[13] There is an indication that British Guiana is itself awakening to the need for exerting itself, in order to bring itself before the notice of a somnolent Mother Country. A deputation arrived in England from the colony in the middle of 1919 charged with the purpose of interviewing the Secretaries for the Colonies and Indian Government, and they went through a course of dinners, meetings and lectures, in which the customary excellent speeches were made. Certain of the speakers made the asservations that British Guiana "could supply all the meat, except mutton, consumed in the Mother Country," and sugar and minerals received equal notice, whilst gold, diamonds and bauxite—an ore of aluminium—were also dangled, metaphorically speaking, before the Imperial-minded diners.

To produce these excellent matters, five thousand settlers per annum are required, the word settler being employed as a well-meaning term for coloured labour. There must be a flow of British capital too. But British capital has not very readily been forthcoming. It can be spared for enterprises anywhere in Spanish America, even "wild-cat" schemes, but not for Guiana, apparently.

[14] *Guiana, British, Dutch and French*, Rodway, South American Series, a most interesting and valuable work.

[15] *Guiana*, op. cit.

[16] *Guiana*, op. cit.

[17] *Peru*, op. cit., where full details are given.

[18] *Ecuador*, op. cit.

[19] *Bolivia*, op. cit.

[20] *Bolivia*, op. cit., where a full account of the rubber industry will be found.

[21]

Total exportation of Brazil in 1906, £52,000,000

Exportation of coffee " " £26,500,000

Exportation of rubber " " £13,300,000

[22] *Brazil*, Pierre Denis, South American Series.

[23] *Brazil*, op. cit.

[24] *Brazil*, op. cit.

[25] This is not the case among the business and commercial circles of Rio and San Paolo, where many of the women are educated in Paris and visit it yearly.—[TRANS.]

[26] *Brazil*, op. cit.

[27] Besides being grown in the great sugar centres, the sugar-cane is a staple crop in Brazil. It is most often used, not for the manufacture of sugar, which calls for a costly plant, but for the production of an alcohol, or sometimes a crude kind of sugar known as *rapa dura*, which is sometimes a kind of molasses, sometimes a sticky cake-sugar.

[28] *Brazil*, op. cit.

[29] *Brazil*, op. cit.

[30] *Brazil*, op. cit.

[31] *Brazil*, op. cit.

[32] The administrative capital is La Plata.

[33] *Uruguay*, Koebel, South American Series.

[34] *Uruguay*, op. cit.

[35] *Uruguay*, op. cit.

[36] *Uruguay*, op. cit.

[37] Pronounced, phonetically, "Who-Who-e," with the accent on the last syllable.

[38] *Paraguay*, Koebel, South American Series.

[39] *Paraguay*, op. cit.

[40] *Patagonia*, Hesketh Prichard, London 1911.

[41] Such, for example, as *South America as an Industrial Field* Koebel, in the South American Series.

[42] Excellent work as regards British trade and general relations was done by the British Diplomatic and Commercial Mission to South America in 1918, under Sir Maurice de Bunsen and Mr. Follett Holt; a Report of which was issued: and some return missions have been sent to England.

[43] Chaves.

[44] Santos-Dumont.

[45] *Can We Set the World in Order: a Science of Corporate Life* (London, 1916). Also *The Tropics: their Resources, People and Future* (Grant Richards, Ltd.).

Milton Keynes UK
Ingram Content Group UK Ltd.
UKHW012312040624
443649UK00007B/573